FAITH AMID THE RUINS

THE BOOK OF HABAKKUK

Other titles in
the Transformative Word series:

FAITH AMID THE RUINS

THE BOOK OF HABAKKUK

TRANSFORMATIVE WORD

HEATH A. THOMAS

Edited by Craig G. Bartholomew

LEXHAM PRESS

Faith Amid the Ruins: The Book of Habakkuk
Transformative Word

Copyright 2016 Heath A. Thomas

Lexham Press, 1313 Commercial St., Bellingham, WA 98225
LexhamPress.com

Print ISBN 9781577997177
Digital ISBN 9781577997184

Series Editor: Craig G. Bartholomew
Lexham Editorial Team: Rebecca Brant, Lynnea Fraser,
    Donna Huisjen, Abby Salinger
Cover Design: Christine Gerhart
Back Cover Design: Brittany Schrock
Typesetting: ProjectLuz.com

*I would like to dedicate this book to Amanda Jill Thomas,
my partner and best friend. We have known the
pain and prayers of Habakkuk over these years.
But we have known the faithfulness of God as
well. I am grateful for you and love you dearly.*

TABLE OF CONTENTS

INTRODUCTION

French philosopher Voltaire held a grudge against the prophet Habakkuk. When questioned by a German scholar about Habakkuk's life, Voltaire quipped, "Sir, you hardly know this Habakkuk; this rogue is capable of anything!"[1]

Whatever the reason for his negativity toward the prophet, Voltaire was wrong. Habakkuk was no rogue. In the prophet's day, destruction and turmoil lay firmly on the horizon. His own people had turned away from God, and the Neo-Babylonian Empire came crushing down on his nation and people. Habakkuk wondered where God was in all of this. He struggled, prayed, and pressed toward God in the midst of catastrophe. Far from being a scoundrel, the prophet is a healthy model of faithfulness to God in the midst of suffering. Habakkuk and his book call us forth to a life of faithfulness to God, even in trying times.

Overview

Habakkuk is a short but powerful prophetic book that uniquely presents an intimate call-and-response format between the prophet and God. No other prophetic book does this in quite the same way, leading Gary

Smith to argue that the book of Habakkuk is akin to a "rare look at the private diary of a confused preacher."[2]

OUTLINE OF HABAKKUK

Oracle (Hab 1:1)

    First complaint (Hab 1:2–4)

    First divine response (Hab 1:5–11)

    Second complaint (Hab 1:12–17; 2:1)

    Second divine response (Hab 2:2–20)

Prayer (Hab 3:1)

    Programmatic introduction (Hab 3:2)

    The divine march to Egypt (Hab 3:3–15)

    The prophet's response (Hab 3:16–19)

Two major sections organize Habakkuk's prayers and God's responses. The first is the "oracle" of Habakkuk, which spans 1:1–2:20. In this oracle, the prophet makes two specific appeals to God.

First, in 1:2–4 he asks God to take notice of the wicked, destructive behavior of his own people. The prophet wants to see the faithful few of his day vindicated by God. In 2:5–11 God responds, but in an unusual way. Instead of directly addressing the prophet's appeal for help, he says that he will, in effect, make matters *worse*. God will raise up the Neo-Babylonian Empire to punish Israel for its sins.

Second, upon hearing this news, the prophet responds in 1:12–17 and 2:1, arguing that God's actions won't help the righteous people as they suffer *now*.

Instead, they will all be wiped out. But the prophet doesn't stop there. Habakkuk argues that, even though God is using them as an instrument of punishment, the Babylonians will not honor God with their actions because they are idol worshipers.

God answers the prophet's second appeal in 2:2–20. In this section God encourages the prophet and his community to be faithful to him because *he* will be faithful to right the wrongs of the world at the appointed time (2:2–5). In 2:6–20 God pronounces a series of "woes" against Babylon that describe the dramatic reversal of fortunes the idolatrous nation will experience. Their fate is sealed. God will punish his own people at the hands of Babylon, to be sure (1:5–11), but the Israelites' punishment will not be the final word. The Babylonians, too, will be judged for their sins (such as pride, idolatry, and their exploitation of other nations), as the woes describe. God encourages his people to be faithful to him despite impending destruction. This uplifting word is typified in 2:4: "Look! His spirit within him is puffed up; it is not upright. But the righteous shall live by his faithfulness." God encourages faithfulness to the end.

Habakkuk 3 is a prayer ascribed to the prophet—his final response to God. In this prayer Habakkuk turns from lament to praise, vowing confidence and trust in God even in the darkest of times. God's encouragement in 2:4 is the foundation of the prophet's stalwart faith. Habakkuk's radical trust is crystalized in the closing words of the book: "Yahweh, my Lord, is my strength; he makes my feet like the deer; he causes me to walk on my high places" (3:19).

TIMELINE OF EVENTS RELATED TO THE BOOK OF HABAKKUK

630 BC: Assyrian power begins to wane in Judah with the death of Assyrian King Ashurbanipal.

616 BC: Egypt sends troops north to ally with Assyria against the rising Neo-Babylonian threat.

609 BC: Egyptian King Necho II kills Judaean King Josiah at Megiddo.

609 BC–597 BC: Judaean King Jehoiakim succeeds Josiah, essentially placed on the throne by Necho II.

605 BC: The Neo-Babylonian Empire gains power in the region of the Levant with King Nebuchadnezzar's victory over Egypt at the Battle of Carchemish.

603–601 BC: Judaean King Jehoiakim pays tribute to Nebuchadnezzar as a vassal of the Neo-Babylonian Empire.

600 BC: Jehoiakim withholds tribute.

597 BC: Nebuchadnezzar lays siege to Jerusalem and captures the king and the elites (Jehoiakim, Ezekiel, Daniel, etc.), deporting them to Babylon.

597–587 BC: Nebuchadnezzar places Zedekiah on the throne of Judah after Jehoiakim and his successor, Jehoiachin, who ruled for only three months.

587 BC: Nebuchadnezzar lays siege to Jerusalem after Zedekiah's rebellion, ultimately destroying the city and leaving it in ruins.

Historical Background of Habakkuk

Habakkuk most likely lived in the final decades of the southern kingdom of Judah. We know this because of the mention of the rise of the Chaldeans (or Babylonians) in Habakkuk 1:6. The rise of the Neo-Babylonian Empire during Habakkuk's day falls in the latter third of the seventh century BC.[3]

Habakkuk saw his kingdom and people falter in their fidelity to God. Judaean King Josiah instituted reforms designed to restore the worship of the one true God among the people of Judah (641–609 BC; see 2 Kgs 22–24), but he died at the hand of the Egyptian Pharaoh Necho II in 609 BC. After Josiah's death, the Egyptians had a hand in placing King Jehoiakim on the throne of Judah, where he reigned from 609–597 BC. In this timeframe Habakkuk saw a decline in his people's fidelity to the true God of Israel. Based on the dark, negative tone of Habakkuk 1:2–4, it is most likely that Habakkuk's prophecies fit within the general time period of Jehoiakim's reign. In this waning phase of the Judaean kingdom, the prophet gets a fresh word that God will bring judgment against his people and city and that this judgment will be a "work" no one will believe (1:5).

The rise of Babylonian power in the land of Palestine came about in part based on their victory over the Egyptians at the battle of Carchemish in 605 BC. Once they had defeated their Egyptian rival, the Babylonians began to make advances against Judah and the land of Palestine, eventually making Judah a vassal state. Once Judah stopped paying tribute to Babylon, however, a progressive set of punitive actions was taken against the vassal state: the initial deportation of elites in Judah (597 BC), subjugation, and ultimately destruction of the capital city of Jerusalem and the razing of the holy place (587 BC).

Habakkuk sees the coming destruction and wonders how God can use *this* nation to judge Judah. After all, the Babylonians will ascribe honor not to God but to their own false gods (Hab 1:15–17). God answers with a vision of encouragement described in 2:2–5. This message concerns God's intervention at the "appointed time" (2:3), when God will right the wrongs of the world, punish the Babylonians, and vindicate his people. Historically, we know that the Persians usurped the Babylonian kingdom by the mid-sixth century BC and that God restored the land (at least in part) to his people, according to the testimony of the later prophets Haggai–Malachi (see specifically Zech 1–3; see also 2 Chr 36).

The Theological Center of Habakkuk

The book of Habakkuk teaches both the faithfulness of God and what faithful living before God looks like when life is turned upside down and catastrophe strikes. God's people had turned against him, and violence and oppression surrounded Habakkuk. But in the midst of that upheaval, God commanded the prophet to live faithfully, even if it cost much. That was fine for Habakkuk, we readily concede. But if God were to give such a directive to *us*, how would we respond? Faith in God and faithfulness to him are demanding!

This is because the call of God upon human life is absolute. Consider Paul's image in Romans 12:1–2, where

> The book of Habakkuk teaches both the faithfulness of God and what faithful living before God looks like when life is turned upside down and catastrophe strikes.

the apostle uses the image of a "living sacrifice" to describe what it means to lovingly serve the Lord Christ. As Jesus voluntarily relinquished his life in death as a sacrifice, so Paul calls upon believers to give themselves over to God in sacrifice: a kind of death! The difference is that in this "death" we become fully alive—the source of Paul's paradoxical image.

So Peter Stuhlmacher summarizes: "Only when they really serve God with their soul, understanding, heart and hands, in other words, always and everywhere, will Christians do justice to their creator and the merciful God who saves them."[4]

Habakkuk reminds us that the act of giving ourselves over, wholly and fully, to the Lord is not an empty pursuit. Life comes about through—and even in a real sense rises from—death. God is faithful to give life to those who respond to his call. Because of this dual emphasis upon faith and obedience to God, Habakkuk teaches what it means to live faithfully before God, even through tragic or confusing times. This book teaches that living faithfully before God is possible only because of the faithfulness *of* God, and Faustin Ntamushobora reminds us that God's people can move from trials to triumphs.[5] God will vindicate those who follow him faithfully, even through suffering: "The righteous will live by his faithfulness" (Hab 2:4).

God often asks people to follow him without providing the next steps. He asked Abram to follow him "to the land that I will show you" (Gen 12:1), and he directed Paul to venture even to the ends of the known world to proclaim the gospel of Jesus Christ. This was a step-by-step process in which God revealed the next step only after each particular step of obedience was completed. Still today God makes extraordinary and difficult demands, just as he asked Habakkuk to live faithfully and incrementally before him, even if the prophet did not know precisely what would happen next.

Following God step by step is never easy. Living by faith sounds doable in the short run, but when the unpleasant realities of life come crashing in, we wonder whether it would have been easier to cling to security and stability. I remember when my wife and I moved from America to England as a newly married couple, believing God to have called us there to study, live, and work. We followed his direction one footfall at a time until we found ourselves in the center of the Cotswolds, a beautiful area in the United Kingdom. Even so, after about five months we wondered whether it would have been easier to stay closer to home! No family around, a sick baby, and English weather made for some tough days. Would it not have been better to remain within the security of our status quo?

Looking back, we can confidently say that it was—and still is—better to pace ourselves in step with God. When God calls us to follow him, our best course of action is to follow through in obedience! The apostle Paul called such keeping pace with the Lord "living by faith" rather than by sight (2 Cor 5:7). This is a process of seeing the invisible, so to speak, and living according to that vision. It is an easy thing to talk about objectively but quite another

> When God calls us to follow him, our best course of action is to follow through in obedience.

when you have to do it in the real world. *The center and focus of the book of Habakkuk is living by faith in the light of the faithfulness of God.* In the context of this central teaching, the book of Habakkuk enables us to see and embrace:

1. a helpful response to suffering, especially through prayer;

2. a call to perseverance and fidelity to God through suffering;

3. an encouraging word of hope that God will not let the righteous be forsaken; and

4. God's future promise of setting the world once again to rights.

SUGGESTED READING

☐   Habakkuk 1–3

☐   Hebrews 10:32–39

☐   John 15:1–25

Reflection

Have you spent time reading or thinking about the book of Habakkuk? If so, write down your initial impressions here. Let this be a foundation for further thinking as you work through the book.

_____

_____

_____

Have you ever experienced confusion about what God was doing in your life? Take a moment to record your experience. What did you think? What did you feel? How did you interact with God during this time?

_____

_____

_____

_____

What are your thoughts about God's requiring faith-fulness to himself in the face of suffering?

_____

_____

_____

_____

PROPHECY IN
THE BIBLE

Introduction

Discussions about biblical prophecy sometimes gar-
ner glazed looks or indifferent stares. After I had dia-
logued for a while on the subject with a colleague, he
simply shrugged and remarked, "It isn't straightforward or terribly clear. I just don't get the literature at
all." His statement is not unusual. Biblical prophecy
can be disconcerting, not only for new believers but
even for those who have been Christians for years.
There are many reasons for this, among them:

- the dizzyingly rapid shifts, without warning or
  explanation, that occur between statements of
  God's judgment and of his restoration;

- the jarring language of divine wrath and violence that butts up against our perceptions of
  Jesus and his love;

- the language about God's judgment that seems
  to belie what we know of his universal love for
  all people;

- strange images and metaphors that pervade the literature to communicate God's messages (such as "cup of wrath," "day of the Lord," and "my rock"); and

- historical, geographical, and national references that are unfamiliar to modern readers.

These issues are real; points 2 and 3, in particular, create confusion between ancient and modern interpretations of Scripture against the backdrop of salvation history. God's seemingly strange outbursts of wrath and violence in the Old Testament in part incited the heretic Marcion (second century AD) to separate the Old Testament God from Jesus, as well as Old Testament Scripture from New Testament teaching. Factors we see in the prophets, like divine wrath and judgment, rank for us today as "disturbing divine behavior" that demands some sort of fix before it can be deemed appropriately Christian.[1]

While we would not go as far as the ancient or modern interpreters who see inherent problems in Old Testament prophecy in need of correcting, we would agree that prophecy is a difficult genre to get our arms around! This chapter is intended to give us a general "feel" for the meaning and functions of prophecy. Equipped with this basic skill, we will be better able to read and understand Habakkuk.

Popular Understandings of Biblical Prophecy

In popular culture people generally divide biblical prophecy into basic categories: (1) "end time" predictions; (2) messianic predictions; and (3) random promises for today. Each of these categories has some merit, but, even taken together, they do not comprehensibly capture the breadth of Old Testament prophecy.

End-Time Predictions

Within this mode people understand biblical prophecy as language concerning the "end" of the world. To chart the timing of that anticipated date, I have seen televangelists and pastors produce charts on which appear such categories as "end-times," "the rapture," and "the second coming." When these well-intentioned individuals speak of biblical prophecy, they usually mean *the future end of the world*— the "end times" when Jesus will come back, rescue the Christians, and burn up this present world. This view of prophecy is often associated with the books of Daniel or Revelation or with some particular New Testament passages.

Examples of this view of prophecy abound, especially in North America. One thinks immediately of the book—highly influential in its time—by Hal Lindsay titled *The Late Great Planet Earth*, which has sold more than 15 million copies. Lindsay opens the book—somewhat backhandedly piquing the interest of the would-be reader—by challenging, "This is a book about prophecy—Bible prophecy. If you have no interest in the future, this isn't for you."[2] The author goes on to detail what he sees to be the future events— all of which, he argues, appear in biblical prophecy— leading up to "Armageddon." For proponents of this view, prophecy is predictive testimony in the Bible, specifically enlightening us about the future end time.

The world as it is—so goes the rhetoric—will not survive; to understand biblical prophecy in this light is to comprehend the language of the "late" great planet Earth.

LEFT BEHIND?

A more recent example of this view of biblical prophecy is the Left Behind series of books and films by Tim LaHaye and Jerry B. Jenkins. This series of 11 books appeared from 1996–2004, followed by four other titles on the same theme from these authors from 2005–2007. These offerings are pop culture interpretations of the books of Daniel and Revelation, which most scholars do not find convincing or definitive in light of more comprehensive views of biblical prophecy.

Messianic Predictions

Historically, the Christian Church has not held such a view of biblical prophecy; the Church has overwhelmingly viewed the Old Testament prophetic works as time-specific promises or predictions concerning the then-coming messiah, Jesus Christ. A number of texts come to mind, such as Isaiah 7:14 as a promise about a special kingly birth that has since been fulfilled in the virgin birth of Jesus (as recorded in the Gospel of Mathew). Another example is the prophecy of the Suffering Servant of Isaiah 53 as a pledge to God's people that a sufferer would atone for the sins of Israel; this was fulfilled in the suffering of Jesus on the cross (Mark 9:31; 10:45; Rom 4:25; 1 Cor 15:3–5; Phil 2:8; Heb 9:28; 1 Pet 2:22–25). In both of these examples, the Old Testament prophecy predicts the coming messiah, which the New Testament recognizes and affirms as Jesus of Nazareth.[3] The Old Testament contains many explicit messianic prophecies, although not all Old Testament prophecies are explicitly messianic.

Promises

Still others interpret biblical prophecies as promises from God. In this vein of interpretation, Old Testament prophecies are promises of the faithfulness of God or "slogans" that we can hold on to in times of trouble. For example, consider the well-known and loved text of Jeremiah 29:11: "'For I know the plans that I *am* planning concerning you,' *declares* Yahweh, 'plans for prosperity and not for harm, to give to you a future and a hope.'" This is one of the verses my mother has claimed as a promise for me for years. Would I call her approach to interpreting Jeremiah 29:11 misguided? No. This is a word we can embrace today, but we would do well to understand how this time-specific promise originally functions in the book of Jeremiah before appropriating it for our day.

In short, biblical prophecy does contain both predictions and promises, so it is not wrong to think about prophecy in either of those ways. But it is more beneficial to see how the predictions and promises fit within the scope and context of a particular prophetic book. Only then will we begin to catch a glimpse of how specific predictions or promises can have any bearing on the Church and the world of our day.

Basic Forms of Prophetic Speech

We have seen that biblical prophecy is predictive; contains promises; and, in particular, reflects messianic expectations. Each such point falls within one or the other of two basic forms or categories of prophetic speech: Predictions or promises of hope (including messianic predictions) appear in messages of salvation, while predictions or promises of judgment appear in messages of God's wrath. From this we can discern two basic forms of speech in biblical prophecy:

1. *Woe oracles*: messages about God's impending or future *judgment* against people or nations. Woe oracles occur in Habakkuk 2:6–20.

2. *Salvation oracles*: messages about God's impending or future *salvation* for people or nations. The key salvation oracle in Habakkuk occurs in 2:2–4.

The book of Habakkuk contains messages of judgment and of salvation related to the people of Israel and to the nation of Babylon. There are no clearly *messianic* prophecies in Habakkuk, as there are in Isaiah 53. But there are words of comfort and hope— assurances that provide the ground for God's people to "wait" on his salvation and remain faithful to him (Hab 2:2–5).

Prophets and Prophecy

Biblical prophecy originates with God, who gives messages to a prophet. A prophet is a spokesperson for God, one who declares God's ways and words to a particular people. In the Bible, prophets can be either men or women. Prophets could come from any stratum of society, whether the royal house (e.g., Isaiah), the priestly families (e.g., Haggai, Zechariah, and perhaps Habakkuk), or the farming community (e.g., Amos).

> ### FEMALE PROPHETS
>
> We are most familiar with the male writing (as opposed to merely speaking) prophets because their books bear their names: Isaiah, Jeremiah, Ezekiel, and Habakkuk, for example. But there is clear scriptural evidence for female prophets as well: Miriam (Exod 15:20–21), Deborah (Judg 4–5), Isaiah's mother (Isa 8:3), and Huldah (2 Kgs 22:14), for example.

According to the teaching of Deuteronomy, prophets were to speak only what God gave them to speak (see Deut 13 and 18). It might be tempting to suppose that God relayed to his prophets spontaneous, word-for-word speeches when they were under some form of trance or divine possession, but that is not usually how prophetic speech works. Prophets were "carried along by the Holy Spirit" (2 Pet 1:21), and they did use a traditional set of speech patterns to communicate God's messages. For this reason, prophetic preaching could be considered a learned form of communication, although the individual personalities and creative styles of the prophets shine through as well.

Prophetic Books

Not all prophets wrote books (Elijah and Elisha in 1–2 Kings, for example, did not, nor did Nathan in 2 Samuel), but many did (Isaiah, Jeremiah, Ezekiel, and our prophet Habakkuk, for example). Both they and their followers composed their messages and compiled them into books. Understanding this is important for a number of reasons, but here we focus on two of them.

First, as we read prophetic books it's important to remember that we are not getting the equivalent of a video recording of what happened in the lives of the prophets. Rather, the books that bear their names are composite collections that speak a unified message. This is true of the prophet Habakkuk. We see that chapter 3 is a prayer, most likely added to Habakkuk's earlier prophetic messages. It is possible that each portion of the book originally appeared at a distinct time in the prophet's life.

Second, as we interpret the prophetic books, we should focus on the overall message of each book rather than slicing and dicing it into disparate parts. The focus of our interpretive effort should be on understanding the message of the book, which has, after all, been handed down to us to read!

Prophecy and the Future

Biblical prophecy is concerned with the future, but perhaps not in the way we might expect. God spoke to prophets so that each of them in turn might speak a particular word to a particular people at a particular time. We call this "forth-telling." Because of God's disdain for injustice in society, he would commission a prophet to speak to those committing the injustice. In the prophetic books God decries many practices in an unjust society, such as slavery, abuse, idolatry, misappropriation of land, slander and lying, sexual misconduct, or defrauding people. For example, God called Amos to preach a word about the injustice being perpetrated *by* God's people *against* God's people and to encourage the oppressors to turn from their sin: "Let justice roll down like water; and righteousness like an ever-flowing stream" (Amos 5:24).

In the New Testament, the "gift" of prophecy the Apostle Paul describes is similar to this prophetic act of "forth-telling." He addresses this in a number of places, but note, for example, Romans 12:6, 1 Corinthians 12:10, and 1 Corinthians 14:1–22. The delivery of a "prophetic word" in the context of a local church conveys a current and relevant word God gives through the believer speaking that word—often to rebuke the church for sin but also to instill comfort. But all prophetic speech is rooted in love, so that God's people can know Jesus Christ and grow in their love for and obedience to him.

> All prophetic speech is rooted in love, so that God's people can know Jesus Christ and grow in their love for and obedience to him.

Alongside "forth-telling" in the Old Testament, prophecy includes "foretelling"—a kind of future-oriented word from God to a community. For those in Bible times who suffered under oppression, a word of foretelling provided encouragement and hope. We see an example in Habakkuk 2:2–4, where God encourages his people to wait for his future salvation, because he would not delay in punishing the wicked and vindicating the faithful. At the same time prophetic foretelling sealed the doom of the oppressors. We see other examples in the various woe-oracles in 2:5–20.

But there is a more expansive kind of foretelling that envisions an ultimate, cosmic future. This kind of prophetic word paints a picture of God's final reconciliation of all things: a complete renewal of the world in conjunction with judgment against sin and evil. This is the cosmic and eschatological sense of the future in biblical prophecy. Habakkuk 2:2–4 can be construed in this way, especially since the vision of 2:2–3 is of the "appointed time" and the "end." This is how the writer of Hebrews interprets these verses: He sees the end as the time when Jesus will come back to redeem all things to himself (Heb 10:36–39).

Prophecy and Jesus

Biblical prophecy in the Old Testament declares God and his ways. So if you want to understand biblical prophecy, you must understand what God says in prophetic speech. Who is this God who gives messages to the prophet? What does the prophetic message tell us about the Lord? What are God's plans? What is the fate of the wicked or of the righteous in the plans of God conveyed here? Each of these questions pushes us more closely to an understanding of the God who speaks.

God spoke through the prophets to proclaim the coming of his kingdom, synonymous with the coming of his Son, the messiah Jesus Christ. So the writer of Hebrews says:

> Although God spoke long ago in many parts and in many ways to the fathers by the prophets, in these last days he has spoken to us by a Son, whom he appointed heir of all things, through whom also he made the world, who is the radiance of his glory

and the representation of his essence, sus-
taining all things by the word of power
(Heb 1:1–3).

This text teaches two truths about the relationship
between Jesus and biblical prophecy. First, Jesus is the
true prophet who discloses the purposes of God.
If God spoke through the prophets in the past, he gave
his people the sure and true, final prophet in his Son,
Jesus! Even though most people rejected Jesus, the
crowds began more and more to recognize him as a
true prophet (Matt 21:11; compare 14:15; 16:14).

CONSUMMATE TRUE PROPHET

Typical of a legitimate prophet from God, Jesus received little honor in his own hometown. Religious
leaders castigated him for his faithfulness to
the Word of God (one need only think of Elijah
or Jeremiah as an effective forerunner of Jesus
from the Old Testament). Again typical of a true
prophet, Jesus spoke of God's salvation coming
through repentance and belief in his reign, as
well as of God's judgment if people were to re-
ject that reign. As the final prophet and ultimate
Word from God, Jesus is the One of whom the
Father said, "This is my beloved Son, with whom
I am well pleased. Listen to him!" (Matt 17:5).[4]

Second, Jesus is the fulfillment of Old Testament
prophecy. Luke and Acts in particular present Jesus
as the One who fulfills the kingdom of God, the
work of God, and the messianic expectation in Old
Testament prophecy. The popular tendency to read

Old Testament prophecy as messianic is absolutely correct. Two points should be noted here:

1. The coming of Jesus as messiah climaxes God's redemptive work with creation, as indicated by Old Testament prophecy (see Isa 60–65).

2. Jesus as the fulfillment of prophecy is not fully comprehensible unless we understand what God is doing in his world.

PRACTICAL GUIDELINES FOR INTERPRETING PROPHECY

A helpful process for interpreting biblical prophecy is as follows:

1. Read the prophetic book closely. Pay attention to the historical background, language, genre, and structure.

2. Identify the overall theological message or messages of the book.

3. Contextualize the message(s) within the larger story of Scripture. This occurs at two levels:
    A. How does the prophetic book fit within the prophets and the Old Testament?
    B. How does the prophetic book fit within the overarching story of Scripture, from creation to new creation?

4. Identify how the message(s) helps us understand:
    A. God (Father, Son, and Holy Spirit);
    B. the world (the created world, what has gone wrong, what God has done to set it right, and where it is headed); and
    C. the Church (the identity, ethics, and future of the people of God).

It is this second point that stands out for interpreting Habakkuk's prophecy. Although there are no explicitly messianic prophecies in Habakkuk, we get a sense in the book of God's ultimate salvation for the righteous and judgment of the wicked. The New Testament writers understood clearly that Jesus is the center of God's work of salvation and judgment. Once we comprehend that message in Habakkuk, we will see how Jesus fits into the picture.

> Although there are no explicitly messianic prophecies in Habakkuk, we get a sense in the book of God's ultimate salvation for the righteous and judgment of the wicked.

SUGGESTED READING

- ☐ Habakkuk 1–3
- ☐ Hebrews 1:1–4; 2 Peter 1:20–21
- ☐ Luke 24

Reflection

How have you understood the concept of biblical prophecy in the past? Write down some of your impressions. What have you learned about it from the discussion in this chapter? Let this be a foundation for further thinking as you work through the book.

_____

_____

_____

_____

_____

What are the messages of salvation and judgment, respectively, in Habakkuk 1–3?

_____

_____

_____

_____

Describe in your own words Jesus' role as the fulfillment of biblical prophecy.

_____

_____

_____

_____

A PORTRAIT OF HABAKKUK

Introduction

Habakkuk is an unusual character in the Bible. Unlike many of the other prophetic books, the opening lines of the prophecy do not tell us when or where he lived or anything about his family (compare Hos 1:1; Amos 1:1; Mic 1:1; Nah 1:1; Zeph 1:1; Hag 1:1; Zech 1:1). His name and background do not appear elsewhere in the Bible either, leaving him somewhat of a nebulous figure. Maybe this explains in part why Voltaire held a grudge against him!

One extrabiblical text, *Bel and the Dragon*, presents Habakkuk with fantastical detail. In this Jewish addition to the book of Daniel, the prophet Daniel is in Persia, imprisoned in a den with seven lions (see Dan 6). This is not a good place to be, but God protects Daniel for a number of days. God sends an angel to provide him a meal, which comes from Habakkuk, who lives in the land of Palestine. The text has it that Habakkuk packs a lunch and is on his way to work in the fields when an angel appears and instructs him to give Daniel some food. Habakkuk points out to the angel that he doesn't know the location of Daniel, Babylon, or the lions' den, so he cannot go. Not to be dissuaded, the angel picks up Habakkuk by the hair and flies him to the den where Daniel waits. Habakkuk delivers the food to Daniel, who is satisfied, after which the angel flies Habakkuk back to Palestine.

In the ancient Jewish text *The Lives of the Prophets*, Habakkuk, a priest from the tribe of Simeon, regularly made visits to the fields (note the similarity to *Bel and the Dragon*). According to this text, when the Babylonians invaded Jerusalem, Habakkuk fled to Egypt but later on returned to Palestine. *The Lives of the Prophets* also indicates that Habakkuk prophesied the destruction and restoration of the temple and the ultimate vindication of God's people.[1] These ancient Jewish texts demonstrate the way in which people tried to fill in the gaps about Habakkuk's life beyond what's included in the Bible.

A more productive way to get to know Habakkuk is by reflecting on his experiences with God throughout the book. Its portrayal of the prophet, as we see through this filter, is real and raw. We don't know whether Habakkuk actually interacted with Daniel or had a special revelation concerning the future of the temple, but we do see a prophet in a difficult place who cries out to God and in the process of relating to him learns a deeper level of devotion. It is possible to think of Habakkuk's experience as a journey of transformation from faith to a deeper level of faithfulness. We are invited to join in this journey.

The Praying Prophet

As noted earlier, the 18th-century philosopher/historian Voltaire joked about the prophet Habakkuk and his impiety. Voltaire believed that "Habakkuk smelt too strongly of brimstone" to be tolerated by pious Protestants.[2] Why would he have pictured Habakkuk as being more hellish than holy? This may have been because Habakkuk speaks to God in a way that may be uncomfortable for believers: uncensored, confrontational, and brutally honest.

> Habakkuk speaks to God in a way that is uncomfortable for believers: uncensored, confrontational, and brutally honest.

We pick up our uneasiness from the tone of Habakkuk's speech; for example, one Jewish midrash (an ancient commentary explaining and expanding upon the meaning of the biblical text) addresses as follows the prophet's words in 2:1:

> Keep your mouth from being rash (Eccl. 5:1) ... When Habakkuk said I will stand on my watch, take up my station at the post (Hab. 2:1) ... This teaches that he drew a form, and stood in its midst. He said 'I will not move from here until You answer me' ... God replied, 'You are not an ignoramous, but rather a Torah scholar!' ... When Habakkuk heard this, he fell on his face and supplicated. He said, 'Master of the Universe! Do not judge me as a wilful transgressor, but rather as an inadvertent

sinner [shogeg].' This is what is written, A prayer of the Prophet Habakkuk. In the mode of Shigionnoth (Hab. 3:1) (Midrash Psalms 7:17).[3]

In this midrash, the prophet is viewed as impudent and rash for speaking as he does to God.[4] It is possible in this light to read the book of Habakkuk as a person's journey from faithlessness to faith (as opposed to one from faith to faithfulness, as earlier noted). According to this interpretation, Habakkuk is doubt-filled and contentious—we might even say cantankerous—failing to trust God because he is experiencing hardship. Habakkuk complains to God, who finally gives his prophet the message recorded in 2:2–20. Once Habakkuk hears this message, so the explanation goes, he turns back to God and regains his faith. Reading the book from this perspective, we see Habakkuk transformed from a less-than-faithful servant into a devout prophet who praises God.

But the reality is different: Habakkuk is a praying prophet who cries out to God in his distress. Habakkuk uses typical, and even formulaic, speech in his cries to God. Frequently in the Old Testament when God's people face injustice, they supplicate with God in prayer and God acts to deliver them based on his love. This pattern is typified in Exodus 2:23–25. The Hebrews faced oppression under Pharaoh and pleaded with God for help. God saw their situation, remembered his covenant with the patriarchs, and determined to deliver them. Remarkably similar language appears in Habakkuk 1:2–3. Note the parallels between the two passages:

They cried out (Exod 2:23)	//	I cry out (Hab 1:2)
He heard (Exod 2:24)	//	But You do not hear (Hab 1:2)
He saw (Exod 2:25)	//	See! (Hab 1:3)
He knew (Exod 2:25)	//	Consider! (Hab 1:3)

These connections demonstrate that Habakkuk uses formulaic language in his time of distress. This is, quite simply, the language of prayer. It is significant that this prayer is hardly an example of faithless speech. Habakkuk appeals confidently to God's ability to see, hear, and understand his people's situation and to do something about it! Just as God has answered his people's prayers in the past, Habakkuk expects him to answer his prayer in the present. Habakkuk's prayer identifies:

1. *His distress*: It is a powerful tool for us as believers to name—to identify and acknowledge—suffering when we encounter it. When distress threatens to overwhelm us, owning our experience—"calling it like it is"—enables us to face it in a manner that allows us to deal appropriately with it. Unacknowledged dis-ease remains in the shadows, a continuous indistinct threat that allows us no way to confront or grab hold of it. Habakkuk clearly names his concern in 1:2–3.

2. *His cry for help*: In his prayer, Habakkuk expresses his angst, clarifying precisely what it is he needs or feels he needs. Identifying a real or

perceived deficit in our lives is healthy. When we decline to express or even recognize and acknowledge our needs, we tend instead to stuff them down. But when we do so, they never go away; they continue to rumble deep inside us until they explode outwardly in some unhealthy way, like a volcano—in need of a venting mechanism—that suddenly erupts. In the life of faith, crying out for help is a way for us to identify and express our needs to God, the One who can do something about them!

3. *His desire for God to act*: It is possible to live a life of quiet resignation to an ambiguous and poorly defined obstacle we call "the will of God." God's will is, of course, a reality to which we as Christians are called to submit. But sometimes in our attempt to be faithful we resign ourselves to God almost as we might to an unbiblical notion of fate; we view God's will as a kind of divine catch-22 waiting in the wings to override or thwart our desires. Habakkuk refuses to yield to "fate." His prayer is prickly and specific, yes, but he is not grousing at God like a defiant child. Habakkuk wants and expects God to act; he calls upon God to do something about wickedness and the wicked, to care for the righteous and to relieve their oppression—to do something on his, and their, behalf!

But why would the prophet suppose that God would act on his behalf? We will uncover this fully in the next chapter when we explore Habakkuk's view of God. For now we can say this: The prophet believes that the Creator is powerful and will act savingly. Habakkuk also understands him to be the covenant-keeping God of Israel. Based on this reality, this identity, God would be true to his covenant with Israel; he would act to save, just as he had done with the Hebrews while they were in Egypt. Habakkuk expected God to answer his prayer because he personally knew the creator-God and the covenant-Lord.

HABAKKUK THE PRIEST?

Scholars have sometimes depicted Habakkuk as a priest. When the prophet says, "I will stand at my post, and station myself on the rampart. And I will keep watch to see what he will say to me, and what he will answer concerning my complaint" (2:1), some identify the language as priestly, since the terms "post" and "rampart" sometimes refer to the temple of God. Also, it is typical of a priest to inquire of the Lord (often in the course of interceding for others) and to await his response.

John Sawyer argues that the structure of lament + oracle (Hab 1:2–11) belongs to temple ritual and indicates that Habakkuk was a priestly prophet.[5] The tradition of Habakkuk being a Levite (as evidenced in *Bel and the Dragon*) further links the prophet to the priesthood. Habakkuk could have been a professional prophet in the service of the temple, as opposed to a country prophet like Amos (see Amos 7:14). It has even been suggested that Habakkuk offered guidance to those coming into the temple with specific life-questions—particularly those dealing with God and justice. But this data is too uncertain to put much weight to it.

From Lament to Praise

Whatever Habakkuk's background, we know from his book that the prophet progresses in his journey with God. I encourage you to read closely Habakkuk's prayers in chapter 1. Do you sense his confusion and anxiety—they're real and palpable! And when God responds in 1:5–11, the prophet's confusion, far from subsiding, only increases. Habakkuk does not have the perspective God does. How could he? He, like us, is a mere mortal! He does not, and cannot, appreciate the full vision of God. But he presses on all the more in his lament, and God gives him the ground for praise. Habakkuk traverses, as one commentator expresses it, from "trials to triumphs."[6]

Habakkuk's transformation is a word of hope and instruction for each of us. He moves from lament (Hab 1) to praise (Hab 3), and we can observe his personal experience recurring again and again in Scripture. This is because God likes to take broken things and mend them—to take hurting people and heal them, confused people and provide guidance, shamed people and honor them, sinful people and forgive them. God's *modus operandi* is typified in the words of David: "You have turned my wailing into my dancing. You have removed my sackcloth and clothed me *with* joy" (Psa 30:11).

> God likes to take broken things and mend them—to take hurting people and heal them, confused people and provide guidance, shamed people and honor them, sinful people and forgive them.

SUGGESTED READING

☐ Habakkuk 1 and 3

☐ Psalm 30

☐ Philippians 2:1–11

☐ 2 Corinthians 1:3–7

Reflection

Read the prophet's prayers of lament in Habakkuk 1. What are your impressions? Are they "over the top"? Would you be able to pray like Habakkuk?

_____

_____

_____

_____

_____

What is your perspective on the transformation of the prophet? Does it bring you encouragement? Does it help you in your own journey with Christ?

_____

_____

_____

_____

_____

Read Philippians 2:1–11 and reflect upon ways in which the movement from lament to praise and from suffering to glory applies, first to Jesus, and then to your own life.

_____

_____

_____

_____

_____

HABAKKUK'S VIEW OF GOD

Introduction

This chapter explores how Habakkuk portrays God and what we can learn from his depiction. Habakkuk provides a specific set of lenses through which we can catch a fresh glimpse of the Lord.

John Calvin famously drew an analogy of the Scriptures as "spectacles." His point was that God provided Scripture to sharpen and focus our understanding of the world. Without the gift of Scripture, our vision would remain distorted or blurred. God's Word corrects our vision so we can live and move effectively in the world.[1]

Calvin's point is good and right, but while affirming it we must also recognize that we may *already* wear another set of spectacles! We did not consciously put on our worldview eyewear; the unique way in which each of us perceives the world derives from our social stratum, family and faith backgrounds, and general experiences, to name only some basic factors. What we may consider natural—whether the issue involves economic policy, politics, sexuality, family dynamics, community life, etc.—is deeply affected by the lenses that are founded in, and supported by, our culture and background. The reason we hold certain views on any topic is that the lenses we wear influence how we see and interpret everything around us. It is altogether possible, even for us as believers, that our view of the world might be shaped by our idolatrous culture rather than by the truth of the gospel of Jesus Christ.

We need, as the Apostle Paul reminds us, the "renewing of our minds" so that we might engage well with the world and other people; we need the light of Jesus to snap our perspective into focus (Rom 12:1–2). The most basic way in which our cultural lenses impact our life is in how we perceive God. Our view of God could be shaped by what we have seen on television or in film; our experience with family or, more specifically, with our father or a father figure; our experience

> We need the light of Scripture to shine on our darkened minds and snap our vision into focus.

of church; or any of a host of other influences. Because our view is so shaped by these lenses, we may miss a true picture of the God revealed in Scripture. We need the light of Scripture to shine on our darkened minds and snap our vision into focus.

For example, some might envision God as a cosmic judge, severe and condescending, perched high up on his heavenly bench weighing from afar the deeds of those depraved defendants—that would be us. One would feel intuitively distant from such a God because he would be completely other; there would be no touch point of connection, no sense of God's empathy, no notion of his compassion for human suffering or limitation, no inkling of his infinite love. This picture of God generates fear: If one does not get life right or find that elusive balance, things will not go well when he or she dies and arrives before God to give an accounting. The eternal balance sheet will reflect that this person's good deeds failed to outweigh the bad ones. And the dour divine judge will render a sentence of damnation. Before the prospect of that final verdict, such a one would live in continual apprehension: Will I ever measure up? Will the judge render a positive or a negative verdict? The danger of this view is that one's daily existence is marked by worry, second guessing, and tentativeness.

Another picture of God is that of an inspector, always peering over one's shoulders to see whether he or she is behaving. If not, God will view the person—his own beloved creation, of whom he had entertained such high hopes—as a severe disappointment. Such a view of God likely generates an extreme sense of anxiety. If one fails to follow the rules, he or she will get it wrong and God will not approve! Others may not approve, either, leading to shunning and terrible disappointment within a church and community. Those proverbial "type A" personalities—whether perfectionists or rule-followers—reading these words may resonate with this picture of God. When one approaches God as the grand inquisitor, one may consider him to be conditional in his love for humanity: For God to truly love someone, the thinking goes, that person must first obey God's rules. Such a performance-based view of life can emerge from seeing

God as a superintendent over one's behavior or a nit-picking micromanager.

Still others may envision God as a kind of absentee landlord. He shows up every once in a while to make sure everything is flowing with reasonable smoothness but otherwise remains unseen unless some egregious problem demands his attention. He simply collects the rent—and even that doesn't have to happen in person! With this view, one does not think much about God at all. He is that ubiquitous presence somewhere in the background, detached from day-to-day living. People with this perception do not experience either the fear that motivates their "God-as-judge" friends or the pervasive dis-ease that grips their "God-as-inspector" acquaintances. They are the independent type, giving the detached deity a nod or a wink here or there but living—under the radar to as great a degree as possible—in a manner that suits their personal preferences, needs, and desires. Church and Bible reading may remain intact as social components of the weekend, and prayer might function as a pastime while one sits in a traffic jam or as a failsafe when one experiences a close call. But for all intents and purposes God has no real impact on day-to-day life: He is preoccupied, aloof, and irrelevant.

Each of these characterizations, and others, can warp our ability to catch the true vision of God in Scripture because on their own they are skewed and incomplete. God reveals himself to humanity through the fullness of Scripture. Each of the above pictures of God presents his truth, but only in a partial way; such distorted perceptions function as caricatures, as one-dimensional line drawings that fail to reveal the gleam of love in God's attentive gaze. Yes, God *is* the cosmic judge who weighs things in the end. God *does* give rules to his people and hold them accountable when they rebel against his ways. And even the last picture presents an element of truth: God is transcendent. But we must never make the mistake of thinking God's transcendence prevents his immanence, his wholehearted investment and involvement in the world he has made. The incarnation of Jesus Christ is a vivid reminder that God condescended in his unfathomable love to take on flesh and dwell among us. Habakkuk 3 presents God as making a journey across the desert to deliver his people from suffering—an image diametrically opposite that of an absentee landlord!

> We must never make the mistake of thinking God's transcendence prevents his immanence, his wholehearted investment and involvement in the world he has made.

The remainder of the chapter delineates Habakkuk's view of God. The prophet lends us his vision as a corrective to any deficiency in our own.

God and Creation

God is not distant from the world he created. Habakkuk teaches a theology of God's fidelity to his creation, and God's devotion comes clearly into view in the prophet's complaint. The complaints in Habakkuk 1:2-4 assume that God *will* counteract violence and chaos precisely because it is *his* creation that has become disordered. If the prophet did not think that God was a caring Lord over his creation, it is sensible to suggest that he would have given up and that Habakkuk would never have voiced his prayer. But the prophet refuses to take this course. Habakkuk recognizes that God fashioned this world with justice (Pss 33:5; 89:15) and knows that the experience of some twisted form of partiality that passes for justice (1:4) is incompatible with God's design and intention for his good world. So Habakkuk's complaint is grounded in a theology of divine commitment to creation.

Notice that Habakkuk does not wish to be delivered *from* the world he inhabits. One temptation for people who try to live faithfully before God is to attempt in one way or another to escape, to cut themselves off from the world. When Christians do this, their underlying desire is to get out of the world. If God could just shuck off this sinking Titanic of an earth, so the thinking goes, then all would be well. But Habakkuk, seeing God's commitment to his created world, instead cries out, "How long?" This prayer appeals to the creator God to work redemptively in the world he has made! The prayer entreats God to rectify the violence of the world. How long must creation suffer before its liberation day? Since, however, Habakkuk sees God as the creator who will redeem his broken world, he prays with fervent hope.

Habakkuk's hope for God's deliverance of creation is reinforced by Charles Spurgeon, the great London preacher. Just as Habakkuk awaits the day when God will deliver the world from sin and injustice, so too did Spurgeon. In his sermon "World on Fire," Spurgeon asserts:

Luther used to say that the world is now in its working clothes and that, by-and-by, it will be arrayed in its Easter garments of joy. One likes to think that the trail of the old serpent will not always remain upon the globe and it is a cheering thought that where sin has abounded God's Glory should yet more abound. I cannot believe in that world being annihilated upon which Jesus was born and lived and died. Surely an earth with a Calvary upon it must last on! Will not the blood of Jesus immortalize it? It has groaned and travailed with mankind, being made subject to vanity for our sake. Surely it is to have its joyful redemption and keep its Sabbaths after the fire has burned out every trace of sin and sorrow.[2]

God *does* address the injustice in his created world; his response to Habakkuk in 1:5–11 and 2:2–20 presents God's "wonder" that will be a step toward the full redemption for his people.

Creation responds to its creator. Habakkuk 3:1–15 depict God's march across the desert to deliver his people, and these verses remind us of the "backstory" of the exodus in the Old Testament. In Exodus 2 God's people cry out to him concerning their experience of suffering in Egypt. Their cry reaches God (who manifests himself in the desert), who marches to deliver them. The sun, moon, seas, rivers, and mountains all respond to their Creator, writhing before him. Notice the language:

When the mountains saw you they writhed;
    a torrent of waters swept by;
the deep gave its voice;
    it raised its hands on high.
Sun *and* moon stood still in *their* place;
    at the light of your arrows they moved about;
    at the gleam of the flashing of your spear.
In fury you marched through *the* earth;
    in anger you trampled the nations.
You went forth for the salvation of your people,
    for the salvation of your anointed (3:10–13).

This poetry reveals how the created order responds to God. As he goes to deliver his people, the world writhes before the God who made it. Why does the world "writhe?" This, as well as the other activity of the created world, is a poetic way to describe how the creation responds and stands at attention to the One who made it. The language here does not mean that the world writhes in agony, but it does stand at attention and respond to the Creator, anxiously anticipating the salvation of God's people, Israel. The presentation is not designed to show that God's people are to be delivered *from the creation* but rather that the created order responds to its Creator as God goes to save his people.

God of the Covenant

Habakkuk 3:13 mentions that God went forth "for the salvation of [his] people." This verse reminds us that Habakkuk teaches a theology of God's fidelity not only to his creation but also to his covenant promises. The Old Testament prophetic books present God as the One who is in special covenant relationship with his people, Israel. The rhetoric of Habakkuk's complaints in chapter 1 works because the poetry addresses *Yhwh*, the covenant name of the God with whom Israel is in covenant relationship. Key texts that explain God's covenant with Israel appear in Genesis 12, 15, 17, and 22; Exodus 19:4–6; and the book of Deuteronomy. It is precisely because God is in covenantal relationship with Israel that Habakkuk is able to pray to *him* for help. As indicated above, the linguistic similarities between Exodus 2:23–25 and Habakkuk 1:2–3 are suggestive: The prophet calls upon the same Lord who has earlier heard the cries of Israel and delivered his people from Egypt (see Hab 3:3–12). Just as he delivered then, *Yhwh*, the covenant God, will deliver his people now.

> Habakkuk teaches a theology of God's fidelity not only to his creation but also to his covenant promises.

The language of *torah* in Habakkuk 1:4 is important to the theology of the book. In the Old Testament, *torah* indicates the instruction of Israel's God (in the legal codes often called the Mosiac law), as well as the wisdom teaching given through God's inspiration (as we see, for instance, in the book of Proverbs). Indeed, Habakkuk appeals to God's covenantal commitment because the *torah* of God has been breached. The prophet's complaint aims at mobilizing God to act on the basis of his divine commitment to his own covenant.

HABAKKUK'S USE OF "TORAH"

The prophet's use of the term indicates that he saw his people as having rejected God's instruction—whether in the general sense of wisdom or in the more specific context of the Mosaic law, or both. On the basis of the stipulations of the covenant, only God can engender change in the hearts of the people ("circumcise" their hearts) and deliver them from their own sin (compare Deut 30:6–10).

The Warrior and Judge

"Yahweh [*Yhwh*] is a man of war; Yahweh is his name" (Exod 15:3). The covenant God of Israel is a warrior who battles the enemies of his people. Habakkuk 3:5 states of God, "Before him went Disease, and Pestilence went out at his feet." This verse reinforces the picture of God as a warrior. In his march to deliver his people, he is accompanied by the plagues, personified as "Disease" and "Pestilence." These are war chiefs that precede God in his military advance toward Egypt. Habakkuk uses this imagery imaginatively, grounding for us the hope that God will do the same for his people with Babylon. If God went out to fight for his people in Egypt, Disease and Pestilence going before him, he will once again fight for them as they languish at the hands of the Babylonians. The picture of God as warrior in Habakkuk 3, then, instills hope in us. This hope is proved in the final verses of this final chapter; the book closes with an affirmation of trust in God.

But God as judge provides a different image from that of the warrior in Habakkuk. As the divine judge,

God weighs the sin of the world, whether such sin derives from Israel or another nation. In Habakkuk 1, the divine judge renders judgment against Israel's sin; he does so by rousing the Babylonians against his own people. In Habakkuk 2, however, the same Judge sentences Babylon, leading to that nation's reversal and downfall. Also in this prophecy, God renders judgment from "his holy temple" (2:20). When he pronounces the verdict, the earth can do nothing but keep silent. God is the cosmic, imperial judge over *all nations and peoples*, and his judgment is just and right.

Conclusion

This chapter has provided the pictures of God that Habakkuk envisions. Still, the one remaining portrait of God we find in Habakkuk is perhaps the most central: that of *the faithful God*, whose fidelity stems from his commitment to both his creation and his covenant. This will be explored in full in chapter 7.

SUGGESTED READING

- ☐ Habakkuk 1–3
- ☐ Exodus 15
- ☐ Psalms 9 and 94
- ☐ 2 Timothy 4:1–8

Reflection

Reflect upon some pictures of God that captivate you. Are they true to the scriptural presentation of God?

_____

_____

_____

_____

Identify connections between the God of creation and the God of the covenant.

_____

_____

_____

_____

Read 2 Timothy 4:1–8 and reflect upon the depiction of Jesus as the judge of life and death, who confers upon his loved ones "the crown of righteousness." How does Jesus fulfill this picture of God from the Old Testament?

_____

_____

_____

_____

5

PROPHECY AND POETRY

Introduction

In almost any translation of the book of Habakkuk, we can see immediately that the lines are broken up into a set of stanzas. The reason is simple: Habakkuk, by and large, is poetry. The book's poetic quality has a bearing on the manner in which we can appreciate and interpret it.

> The book's poetic quality has a bearing on the manner in which we can appreciate and interpret it.

Scholars today debate some of the factors that set apart biblical poetry from prose, but at the most basic level, the Bible's poetry is a repetitive, terse, highly paratactic (juxtaposing phrases or clauses without connectives), and image-rich way of speaking that draws parallels between ideas at the level of the individual poetic line. Prose, by contrast, is less succinct and is built around storytelling and narrative markers (such as extended paragraphs, plot progression, scene changes, etc.); as such, it is less apt to build its communicative strategy around parallel lines.

Terseness and Repetition

Hebrew poetry is short, dense, and rich in imagery. "Terseness" is a word that describes this phenomenon. Note the terse richness of the verse below:

> Why do you cause me to see evil
> > *while* you look at trouble?
> Destruction and violence happen before me;
> > contention and strife arise (Hab 1:3).

In this verse no fewer than six terms are used to describe the terrible situation Habakkuk faces: "evil," "trouble," "destruction," "violence," "contention," and "strife." In the span of two full poetic lines, we see the full range of the prophet's experience of negativity and disorder. Hebrew poetry is all about maximum impact in minimum space.

Repetition also appears in poetry, working in close conjunction with terseness. A good example of repetition at work in Habakkuk appears in chapter 3:

> Yet I will rejoice in Yahweh;
> > I will exult in the God of my salvation.
> Yahweh, my Lord, *is* my strength;
> > he makes my feet like the deer;
> > he causes me to walk on my high places
> > (Hab 3:18–19).

Notice how terms and concepts recur within and across poetic lines, with parallel ideas signified by the sign "//":

I will rejoice	//	I will exult		
Yahweh	//	the God of my salvation	//	Yahweh
My Lord	//	my strength		
He makes my feet	//	he causes me to walk		
Like the deer	//	on my high places		

The poetry works because the repeated element modifies, clarifies, and expounds the originating element. The first descriptor for God is his covenant name, Yahweh (Hab 3:18). The second half of the line modifies and expounds Yahweh's identity: He is "the God of my salvation." The name Yahweh is repeated in 3:19, building upon the divine presentation, but now he is depicted as "my Lord," which is parallel to "my strength." The last two lines of this verse go on to tell us how Yahweh, the God of Habakkuk's salvation as well as his Lord, is the poet's "strength": He enables Habakkuk to ascend the protective heights without falling, much as an agile deer is able to negotiate the rocky terrain around Israel without hurtling to its death. This beautiful affirmation of God and hopeful presentation of faith is achieved through two verses of tightly integrated parallelism.

Imagery

Multiple images, often logically unconnected, have been brought together in Habakkuk. The poetry depicts God in a series of images we have already discussed: creator, warrior, and judge. But we also see how the concept of reversal is achieved through imagery, in particular in the woe-oracles from Habakkuk 2:5–20. In these oracles, the Babylonians are portrayed in a series of negative images, which reinforce the idea that their might will not last. Their power and authority will be subverted as God vindicates the righteous. Again, the poetry communicates this message through a series of images. Babylon is portrayed as:

1. a thief (2:6);

2. a raider (2:9);

3. an unjust builder—the city of blood (2:12);

4. a deficient party host (2:15); and

5. an idolater and idol maker (2:19).

Each woe and each image in its own way presents a great reversal: Thieves will be plundered, unjust

CITY OF BLOOD!

One of Habakkuk's most provocative images is that of an unjust builder who constructs a city of blood (Hab 2:12)! The image of a city constructed in blood was evidently popular among the prophets, recurring as it does in Micah 3:10. The metaphor depicts a profound irrationality that lies at the heart of all such builders: They construct their city based on their own perceived permanence, expecting it to last to perpetuity, but their short-sightedness renders their efforts vain, empty, and ultimately broken! For all their frenetic activity, their work is for naught (Hab 2:13b); they are doomed to imbibe the fatal cup of God's wrath. The image presents a terrible visual that communicates in a way that straightforward description could not.

profits will evaporate, cities built upon bloodshed will experience ruin, those inciting others to drunkenness will be filled with the cup of God's wrath, and those who trust in idols will fall to destruction. The imagery enables communication of the reversal in a striking and memorable way that simple explanation in prose could never capture. The imagery provides a concrete and unforgettable picture of the folly of trusting in anything except God and of the destruction that is coming for those who make this fatal mistake—the Babylonians.

Metaphor

A metaphor is an analogy or association established between disparate notions or ideas. To say that God is a rock, as we see in Habakkuk 1:12, is to use a metaphor to describe God or clarify one of his traits. Metaphor is a terse way of showcasing similarities between the things being compared; it does so without explanation, assuming we will make the connection based on experience. In this case, to say that God is a rock is to say not that God is gray or stony, but that he is stable and strong, a source of shelter or protection. These connotations emerge naturally from the analogy between God and rock. The metaphor, though brief, opens up or expands our conception of God, as opposed to boiling it down to a bare minimum. The use of this particular metaphor provides an economic but highly effective

> To say that God is a rock is to say not that God is gray or stony, but that he is stable and strong, a source of shelter or protection.

way to enable productive reflection upon the nature and character of God as our rock.

Another powerful deployment of metaphor occurs in the same passage, comprised of 1:12–17. In this section, the Babylonians are described as fishermen who pull up nations in their dragnet. The analogy between "Babylonian army" and "fishermen" works not because the Babylonians like to catch or eat fish. Rather, the imagery of Babylon pulling up nations with a "hook" and a "net" instills in our mind an immediate and obvious connection between fishing for food and fishing for people! In this case the analogy enables us to associate ordinary activity (fishing) with unspeakably terrible activity (the invasion and capture of God's people through warfare). Metaphor carries greater punch than straightforward description because it more compactly and strikingly makes the point.

Prophecy and Music

Poetry as a genre is suited for music. Short, dense, image-rich, repetitive lines comprise the stuff of lyrics in popular music of our day, as they have throughout history. Samuel Maier has pointed out that musical notations often occur in prophetic poetry, leading him to argue that poetry, prophecy, and music go hand in hand.[1] Such notations appear as well in Habakkuk: "according to the Shigionoth" in 3:1 and "to the choirmaster with stringed instruments" in 3:19. The precise meaning of "Shigionoth" is unclear, though most scholars think the term is related to instrumentation. Apparently, Habakkuk 3 was set to music and the poetry was sung with musical accompaniment.

If this conjecture is accurate, at least some of the poetry of Habakkuk engaged its original audience sensually beyond an appeal to their sight. Sound is intended to accompany the reading process. And if that sound is musical, it is possible that Habakkuk 3 was sung in worship or liturgical contexts. This is a helpful reminder for us that the prophetic word read, spoken, and sung has very early roots. The worship of God was, from the beginning, likely a multi-sensory experience and encounter with the Lord.

Poetry, Prophecy, and Imagination

This chapter has exposed us to some of the qualities of the poetry in Habakkuk, alerting us that the book is *imaginative* literature. By labeling Habakkuk imaginative I am not suggesting that its content is mythical, nonhistorical, or false. I intend only to say that in a profound way Habakkuk excites us to reflection and creativity through appeals related to sound, structure, and sense.

When the poetry of Habakkuk identifies God as rock or judge or warrior, these metaphorical descriptors stimulate our reflection about what God is like. Description through metaphor opens up our minds to possibilities about God's nature and character, and it does so in non-reductive (open-ended or non-limiting) and evocative ways. Imagination in conjunction with prophecy is not, however, a flight of fancy. Rather, the poetry presents a new way of seeing reality—one in which God and the world are presented and conceived in a new light or from a perspective not previously considered.

> The book's poetry of prophecy imaginatively opens up an unexplored thought-world for us.

The poetry of Habakkuk affords a set of concepts and a vocabulary by which we can negotiate present suffering and move forward in faith. The book's poetic prophecy imaginatively opens up an unexplored thought-world for us. Based on the poetic nature and appeal of the book, we can more readily imagine a better world—a world in which we might live faithfully before our faithful God. The startling imagery reminds us—in ways we will not soon forget—that God will set the world right in the end. We need only to trust in him and live by faith.

SUGGESTED READING

☐   Habakkuk 2 and 3

☐   Psalms 6 and 7:1

☐   Colossians 1:15–20

☐   2 Corinthians 1:3–7

Reflection

Have you thought previously about the importance of poetry in interpreting prophecy? How, if at all, has Habakkuk's poetry helped you to engage his book?

_____

_____

_____

_____

Read Psalm 6. Identify in this psalm the elements of poetry presented in this chapter: terseness, repetition, imagery, metaphor, and imagination. Go through the same exercise with Colossians 1:15–20. What poetic images strike you from these passages? How and why will they stay with you?

_____

_____

_____

_____

Reflect on the concept of God as the artist who has provided imaginative literature like Habakkuk in Scripture. How does your acknowledgment of God's artistic prowess change or deepen your understanding of him?

_____

_____

_____

_____

6

WAITING ON GOD

Introduction

Waiting for anything can be difficult. I sometimes have a hard time waiting a minute or two for my coffee to warm up in the microwave. When I go trout fishing, I first have to travel for a few hours and thus am forced to wait to get started until I have arrived and prepared. Life's "waiting room" can be a frustrating place, especially for us moderns who have to a large extent lost a tolerance for or appreciation of delayed gratification.

Ours is a world of quick or instant oatmeal (we actually have a choice on this one!), instant messages, quick fixes, fast lanes, and turbo taxes. In a culture with little tolerance for the concept of later, waiting may not seem to be a good or beneficial activity (how ironic that we refer to everything we do as "active-ity"). "Patience is a virtue," we've been taught, but we ask ourselves how biding our time or spinning our wheels could possibly enhance our productivity or quality of life. For people accustomed—for the first time in history!—to accessing a plethora of information at the click of a mouse, waiting may seem to be an intrusive inconvenience. Any notion of slowing down—heaven forbid doing so on a voluntary basis!—or of deliberately delaying gratification may be understood as anachronistic and counterproductive, a retreat back to the dark ages or an artificial holding back of the thrusting momentum of progress.

But Scripture reveals that waiting can be a good thing—or, as we might at first glance construe it, at least an inconvenience with a possible upside in terms of patience development. We could take this further, though, using the language of spiritual formation and growth in Christ. In this parlance, waiting—far from being merely a passive imposition—is a kind of *spiritual discipline*. Spiritual disciplines are regular, habitual practices in our lives that are designed to help us develop a closer relationship with God.

In terms of the traditional formulation, 12 spiritual disciplines exist in the Christian life: meditation, prayer, fasting, study, simplicity, solitude, submission, service, confession, worship, guidance, and celebration.[1] Through regular engagement of these inward and outward actions, Christians experience the fullness of God. These are "disciplines" precisely because they require diligent commitment. Habakkuk reveals another discipline implied but not directly included in the 12: that of waiting on God, especially in and through the discipline of prayer.

> Waiting upon God instills in us a new perspective and opens us up to renewed life before him.

In this chapter we will uncover the meaning of waiting upon God, how we go about doing this on a practical level, and what this means for our lives. Perhaps to

our surprise, we will discover that waiting upon God
instills in us a new perspective and opens us up to
renewed life before him. The spiritual discipline of
waiting on the Lord will help us recognize—experientially, not just cognitively—that we are not alone.
This lesson derives from the little book of Habakkuk,
typified in the opening words of Habakkuk 2:

> I will keep watch to see what he will say to
> me, and what he will answer concerning my
> complaint (2:1).

Much can be unpacked from this deceptively brief
verse. The prophet's words teach us that waiting en-
tails three aspects: speaking to God, silence before
God, and receiving God's response. Waiting on God
demands that we first address him in prayer. He has
taken the initiative to speak first to us by means of
his gifts of life and of his Son, Jesus, the giver of life.
Creation testifies to a God who speaks his word of
love to, and remains in communion with, all that he
has made—very much including you and me. God's
commissioning of his Son, Jesus Christ, as suffering
savior, messiah, and king testifies to his identity as a
God who both creates and redeems. And both creation
and redemption speak God's word of love to us. But in
response to his already given Word, we who belong
to him call back to God in prayer. So when Habakkuk
prays and awaits the divine "answer," the prophet is
only carrying forward the conversation God has already begun!

Waiting on God, however, implies actively and
deliberately listening for his response. As Habakkuk
"keeps watch" to see what God will say, silence is

crucial. Prayer involves talking to God, but prayer at its most fundamental level is *listening to God*. Listening well demands silence, and effective use of silence is an exacting process that is not easy to initiate or maintain in a loud world. But stilling ourselves before the Creator so that we can hear *his* Word brings us life. Martin Laird built on the thought of St. John of the Cross when he noted that "silence is an urgent necessity for us; silence is necessary if we are to hear God speaking in eternal silence; our own silence is necessary if God is to hear us."[2] Listening is that act of silence through which we open ourselves up to hear God speak and thereby commune with him.

Waiting on God anticipates his response. God answers prayer. He does so time and again, and he has done so *definitively* in Jesus Christ. In the book of Habakkuk, God answers the prophet's prayers as well. But what happens between the moment when we experience distress and God provides his response and his presence? What about the time of waiting? This deceptively important interval is what this chapter explores.

The Waiting Room

It used to be common for a husband to remain in the hospital waiting room while his wife gave birth. There in the waiting room, he would pace, often crying out to God for the health of his most intimate partner and the safe arrival of their child. Friends and family would gather there as well, all anticipating the happy news.

The hospital waiting room is no longer a reality for a husband because he now most often participates in the birthing room with his spouse. But that does not mean we cannot learn from life's waiting room experiences. The life of faith has a waiting room as well. It's that place from which God's people cry out to him and await his response. Although he may at times seem hidden away, he is in reality actively birthing the new work he has in store. Still, before he discloses his news, those in the waiting room pace, pray, and petition him.

There are at least two facets of the waiting room in the life of faith. It is a place of prayer, a location from which we cry out to God and await his response. Our reason for prayer is multiform and continuous because life is endlessly complex. The waiting room is the place where we pray about a job loss, an illness, a family issue, betrayal, adversity, bereavement, an experience of injustice or abuse, ... and the list goes on endlessly. From the waiting room God's people approach their good heavenly Father and ask him to intervene. We cry from the darkness. And then we wait. For what do we wait? Quite simply, for God and for his answer.

> Our reason for prayer is multiform and continuous because life is endlessly complex.

The call to wait on God pervades Scripture. A sampling:

> Answer me when I call, O God of my righteousness! You have given me relief when I was in distress. Be gracious to me and hear my prayer! (Psa 4:1 ESV).

> Lead me in your truth and teach me, for you are the God of my salvation; for you I wait all the day long (Psa 25:5 ESV).

> May integrity and uprightness preserve me, for I wait for you (Psa 25:21 ESV).

> Wait for the LORD; be strong, and let your heart take courage; wait for the LORD! (Psa 27:14 ESV).

> But for you, O LORD, do I wait; it is you, O Lord my God, who will answer (Psa 38:15 ESV).

> And now, O LORD, for what do I wait? My hope is in you (Psa 39:7 ESV).

Each of these texts represents faithful prayer to God. Sufferers utter these prayers in real situations of distress, reminding us that God wants us to call out to him. Why? Because *God does indeed hear and answer prayer!* These texts remind us that waiting for God and his deliverance remains central to the life of faith. The expectation of divine deliverance is real, but in the present moment of suffering we may not experience it. Hope for God's deliverance is peeking around the corner, implicit in his present work and in what we have come to know of him through his past activity.

Is such expectant waiting on God the go-to recourse for most of us when we face times of trouble? Likely not. Humans exhibit many overt responses to distress, some of which include:

1. *Isolation*: Many times when we suffer from pain—whether the issue be sin, our enemies, our circumstances, sickness, or even a feeling

that God has turned against us—we may be tempted to shut ourselves off from God and others. We may object, "This isn't my burden to bear" or "I'll be embarrassed if others know."

2. *Pretending*: One of the most pernicious responses to pain and suffering, I would argue, is putting on a happy face and pretending to the world that everything is okay, even when we feel ourselves to be dying inside. This is an unhealthy response to pain because it prevents us from dealing with the suffering. In addition, putting on a false front prevents us from receiving help from the community of faith. God created the Church in part so that believers might be present to "bear" one another's burdens (Gal 6:2). It is difficult to do any bearing when people pretend nothing is wrong!

3. *Minimizing*: At times, in a misguided attempt to be faithful to the life of Christ and in response to some apparent injunctions in Scripture (e.g., Rom 5:2-4; Phil 3:10; Col 1:24; 2 Tim 1:12; 1 Pet 1:6-9; 3:8-22; 4:1-19; Jas 1:2; 5:7-10), we might dismiss the pain of the moment as something that is inherently disciplinary. God is *doing something spiritual in us through* the distress, and so we need not complain or really think it is all that bad. Dealing with distress in this way does not face suffering full on but minimizes its importance or impact in our lives. The response from Habakkuk is different. Instead of minimizing pain and distress or explaining it away as something that will build our souls,

Habakkuk faces the distress head on and offers the pain up to God.

Psychological insights show us that such overt actions may derive from deeper and more complex defense mechanisms. Habakkuk leads us away from these unhealthy coping patterns and introduces us instead to *prayer*. Prayer provides us both the space and the context for verbalizing our distress to God. Habakkuk shows us that the first two options (isolation and pretending) are not always possible and that the third (minimizing) is not always advisable. In the first place, Habakkuk refuses to isolate himself from God. Sometimes when we face distress we break away from either God or other people; Habakkuk shows us the foolishness of this idea.

The prayers of Habakkuk also show us that trying to pretend everything is all right is at best insincere and at worst an exercise in denial. A synthetic or skin-deep version of Christian faithfulness is inadequate for a genuine, healthy relationship with God. The prophet's prayers reveal that all is not well in his world. Pretending our problems do not exist denies the brokenness of individual and communal life and prevents God's in-breaking and restorative work in Christ. The hope of prayer is that God will make himself available and work his redemption in a broken world. If we live as though creation does not groan (Rom 8), we devalue the hurt and tears of the

> Pretending our problems do not exist denies the brokenness of individual and communal life and prevents God's in-breaking and restorative work in Christ.

world. Such devaluation prevents us from crying out to God that his kingdom may come and his will be done in this earth as it is in heaven (Matt 6:10).

Despite biblical injunctions to "rejoice in suffering" or to "count it all joy" when we experience pain as discipline, it will not do for us to indiscriminately collapse pain into some indistinct component of joy. Our recognition of the experience of pain as disciplinary, or redemptive, or whatever, is fully gained only *after* we have acknowledged, addressed, negotiated, come to terms with, and walked through our suffering. Christ's suffering is a helpful analogy: He *truly* experienced pain and cried out to God in honest supplication, "My God! My God! Why have you forsaken me?" (Mark 15:34). The vindication of God that is proven through Christ's resurrection arrives after a three-day period of darkness.

Internalizing the implications of this analogy encourages us to experientially discover the hope that God works in *all things* (even pain and suffering) for our good—though that in no way diminishes what may be the tragedy of the present moment. Working through these implications instills within us hope; this process invites us as well to give voice to the experience of pain in and through prayer, as Habakkuk did in Habakkuk 3. Thus joy does not come before the experience of pain but within, through, and after it. Nor does joy *replace* pain.

Pain must be addressed and negotiated prior to our experiencing any form of triumph *over* it. Modeling our prayers after Habakkuk's can prevent us from minimizing our pain or running ahead too quickly to the "resurrection" without fully acknowledging and

> A responsible spirituality allows individuals to hurt and pray through their pain while dealing with it—and with God—in the waiting room.

engaging the suffering that has come along with the crucible we have experienced. A responsible spirituality allows individuals to hurt and pray through their pain while dealing with it—and with God—in the waiting room. A robust spirituality of suffering calls the people of God to allow others to "mourn" (Rom 12:15) and pray about distress without expecting them to transition too quickly to resolution, restoration, or rejoicing.

SHARING HIS SCARS

The scars of Christ have not disappeared. Even after his resurrection the New Testament appearances of Jesus remind us that Jesus still displayed marks of the crucifixion. He showed his followers the wound in his side and the scars in his hands. Jesus' scars memorialize both the tragedy of his crucifixion and the triumph of his resurrection. Likewise, our own scars are often still visible long after we have walked through pain.

Waiting in Hope

It is hard to wait on God. But Habakkuk reminds us that waiting upon God is not an empty hope—not a hope against hope or a vague yearning for a resolution that may or may not actually come—because we know that God *will* act. The spiritual discipline of waiting on God is that of anticipating his work, just as Habakkuk did. Habakkuk knew what God had said concerning his people. Consequently, he was able to wait on God with an authentic, expectant hope.

Habakkuk waited in the hope of God's ultimate restoration of his people. Through the prophet's eyes, we witness the greed of Babylon as they gobble up people and resources with the efficiency of a wood-chipper, spitting out the refuse like a garbled mess of garbage. Babylon's inflated sense of self (2:4a) left them calloused to the collateral damage of their tyranny—an unceasing procession of suffering (1:3). Already in the first four verses of his book Habakkuk lays out questions before God: What was God up to? How did the situations of the world mesh with his plan? These were real questions demanding real answers.

And God did answer. Babylonian tyranny could not survive. Yes, God had sent the Babylonians to invade Judah in the last days of the seventh century BC; these ruthless captors were God's instrument of punishment for his own rebellious people (1:5–11). But after judgment God would restore his people when they repented of their sin and turned back to him (2:2–20).

Habakkuk's response to God was a firm affirmation, not merely of resignation but of hope: "I will wait quietly" (3:16). Habakkuk waited upon God with a genuine, pregnant hope. Waiting in hope is not like seeing a mirage in the sands of the desert—"present" one moment and gone the next. Waiting with hope is based upon a certainty that God has spoken and will act. The prophet Isaiah expresses it this way:

> But those who wait for Yahweh shall renew
> *their* strength.
> They shall go up *with* wings like eagles;
> they shall run and not grow weary;
> they shall walk and not be faint (Isa 40:31).

Like Isaiah, Habakkuk hopes in God with confidence. Even in the face of impending invasion by the Babylonians, the prophet affirms.

> Though the fig tree *does* not blossom,
>> nor there be fruit on the vines;
> the yield of *the* olive tree fails,
>> and the cultivated fields do not yield food;
> *the* flock is cut off from the animal pen,
>> and there is no cattle in the stalls,
> Yet I will rejoice in Yahweh;
>> I will exult in the God of my salvation.
> Yahweh, my Lord, *is* my strength;
>> he makes my feet like the deer;
>> he causes me to walk on my high places
>> (Hab 3:17–19).

This is a most extraordinary affirmation! Waiting for destruction, yet with feet set "on my high places." Why could the prophet speak this word of hope? How was it that he could simply wait for destruction? Because God's ultimate deliverance was his hope.

Hope in Jesus

God's restoration envisioned by Habakkuk began in the prophet's day but came to ultimate fruition in the advent of Jesus. According to Paul in the book of Romans, Jesus' incarnation and work comprised the climax of God's plan for restoring the brokenness and rebellion of the world (see, for example, Rom 8). Against the kinds of issues about which Habakkuk complained—tyranny, injustice, hatred, abuse, greed, and lies—God proclaimed a final *no!* in Jesus. When Jesus offered his life on the cross he defeated death and sin and inaugurated his new creation. This new life is not just for humanity but also for the entirety of the created order. In Jesus' own words he will make "all things new" (Rev 21:5).

Our hope is found in what the Father has done through Jesus (Col 1:15–20). In him all of this world *will be* finally restored. And those who have faith in him will live with him. His followers will experience no more tears, death, tyranny, deception, or nature that may be characterized as "red in tooth and claw."[3] His followers *will* experience real peace for the real world. Hope in Jesus is not vapid.

But until our Lord makes all things new, suffering continues and pain persists. How do God's people live faithfully in the meantime? By faith. We wait in hope and remain faithful to God until the end. So the writer of Hebrews encourages:

> For you have need of endurance, in order that after you have done the will of God, you may receive what was promised. For yet:
>
> "a very, very little *while*,
>   *and* the one who is coming will come and will not delay.
> But my righteous one will live by faith,
>   and if he shrinks back, my soul is not well pleased with him."
>
> But we are not among those who shrink back to destruction, but among those who have faith to the preservation of our souls (Heb 10:36–39).

SUGGESTED READING

- ☐ Habakkuk 1 and 3
- ☐ Hebrews 10
- ☐ Romans 8
- ☐ Psalms 38 and 39

Reflection

When have you found yourself in the "waiting room" of life? Write down your experiences.

_____

_____

_____

_____

Do you identify with any unhealthy responses to distress, such as minimizing, pretending, or isolation? Are there other unwholesome responses you exhibit, such as substance abuse or other forms of escape?

_____

_____

_____

_____

In practical terms, how can you build healthy practices into your life that will allow you to "wait on God"? Will you devote time in prayer to a particular issue? Will you build reflective space into your schedule to help you process pain?

_____

_____

_____

_____

FAITH IN THE FAITHFUL GOD

Introduction

> My mouth will tell of your righteousness,
> your salvation *all day long*,
> though I do not know *the full* sum *of them*
> (Psa 71:15).

The verse above testifies to Israel's God and to his "righteousness" and "salvation." The psalmist prays to God for help, and by the time we arrive with him at this verse God has apparently answered the prayer with salvation. The language the psalmist uses to describe God's deliverance, his act of salvation, is "righteousness." In Scripture, and especially in the Old Testament, the "righteousness of God" is a concept that speaks to God's saving deeds. That is how the psalmist intends "your righteousness" in the verse. Because God has saved, the psalmist can recount God's righteousness to others. Peter Stuhlmacher rightly summarizes:

> In the Old Testament and early Judaism,
> God's righteousness thus means the activity

of God through which he creates well-being and salvation in history (specifically that of Israel), in creation, and in the situation of the earthly or eschatological judgment.[1]

The book of Habakkuk reveals God's righteousness: his faithfulness and salvation. This is crystallized most clearly in the profound teaching from Habakkuk 2:2–5. This chapter will explore that foundational text and uncover its reception in the New Testament, particularly in Romans 1:17; Galatians 3:11; and Hebrews 10:36–39. From this chapter we gain a deeper and richer appreciation for the God of faithfulness, though we cannot hope to measure its full sum and implications!

Habakkuk 2:2–5

In these verses, God explains what it means to live by faith. In Habakkuk 1:12–17 the prophet asks how God can use idolatrous Babylon to do his bidding. Babylon not only refuses to honor God, but will take actions against God's people that will far outstrip God's design: Their act of punishment, Habakkuk complains, will exceed the crime. The prophet "takes his stand" to see how God will respond (Hab 2:1).

God replies in 2:2–5 through a vision designed to afford comfort and hope, even in the face of Babylonian invasion, to the prophet and the people he represents. Babylon's invasion will be terrifying, but God will be his people's source of hope. Further, the vision testifies that God will overthrow the wicked and vindicate the righteous, as 2:6–20 confirms. The vision proclaims that the final vindication will take place in the future; God describes it as occurring at an appointed time—at the "end." But even if fulfillment seems de-layed, God's people should wait expectantly (2:3).

How should God's people, then and now, live before him as they wait for his ultimate salvation? Habakkuk 2:4b provides the answer: "But the righteous shall live by his faithfulness." The most adequate explanation of this much-discussed verse incorporates three inter-related points:

1. *God is faithful to his people.* The verse confirms that God is faithful to punish the wicked and vindicate the suffering righteous. His faith-fulness to his faithful people is real, even if they suffer now under the weight either of wicked Israelites (see Hab 1:2–4) or of wicked Babylonians (see Hab 1:5–17). Because God de-clares that he will do so, we know that the vi-sion is reliable—and that, by extension, God's word is reliable.

2. *The verse highlights a contrast.* Most commenta-tors recognize that it contrasts a prideful soul—one who is "puffed up," "defiant," and "arrogant" (see Hab 2:4–5)—with the "righteous." The righ-teous individual will "live," while the proud will fall. What is unclear is the identity of the haughty. Is the reference to the Babylonians or to the faithless Israelites who abandon faith on the assumption that God has abandoned his people? Either reading is possible, though the Hebrew renderings seem to lean toward the faithless Israelite who shrinks back from God. The Old Greek translations, on the other hand, suggest that it is the egotistical Babylonians

who will experience utter ruin. Either way, in contrast, the righteous will live.

3. *God expects faithfulness from his people.* The verse clearly anticipates Israel's obedience and faithfulness to God. God is faithful to his people, to be sure. But that does not imply that the Israelites should simply bide their time as they wait for him to enact their salvation. No, the verse clearly expects faithfulness from the people toward God. What would this look like, practically speaking? To begin with, they should look to and trust God's word (the vision) and wait for God to make good on that word. Second, they are to live lives that are pleasing to God in all possible ways, regardless of the level of hindrance or difficulty.

These three points highlight the inter-effective manner in which divine and human faithfulness work in the Christian life. First and foremost, God remains faithful; he saves, delivers, redeems, forgives, and sets humanity on the path before him. But in response to God's faithfulness, we who are in Christ are to live in obedience to him. Although we cannot earn our way to God's favor through good deeds, God has gone to the distant country on our behalf because of his great love for us. He has bought us back from our destitution and helpless state. God's faithful people act in love

> Although humanity cannot earn our way to God's favor through good deeds, God has gone to the distant country on our behalf because of his great love for us.

in response to God's already given and already revealed love. Habakkuk 2:4 calls for a decision. Shall we who know the love and faithfulness of the Lord remain loyal to our king, or shall we shrink back, falling into unbelief and sin?

This verse also emphasizes the idea of living—but what kind of life does Habakkuk have in mind? The exact nature of the life envisioned in 2:4b actually remains poorly defined. The text may indicate that the righteous will not be swept away in the Babylonian onslaught but will instead be exiled, remaining physically alive in a foreign land. This understanding of life parallels the theological thought process of Habakkuk's contemporary, the prophet Jeremiah. In Jeremiah 31:1–6 God affirms that he will bring his people back to Zion. God has punished them with the sword but pledges in Jeremiah 31:4, "I will build you up again and you will be built, O Maiden Israel" (author's translation). He will gather his people from the ends of the earth and resettle them in his place, under his rule, and as his people. If this is a fertile co-text, it illumines the nature of life as envisioned in Habakkuk 2:4b, revealing that God will not utterly destroy his people for their sin but will rather preserve a remnant that will be purified through the fires of judgment. Life is a manifestation of the grace of God as he preserves Israel in salvation through the crucible of judgment.

And yet with a little imagination it is not difficult for us to envision a broader understanding of the life that is here envisioned. In light of the teaching in Habakkuk 2:2–3 that the vision concerns the "end," the meaning of "life" in 2:4b may indicate a kind of resurrection—an idea that, though it may seem pre-mature, is not unheard of in the Minor Prophets. For example, in Hosea 6:1–2 God tells his people that though they will die in exile, they will be "revived": "He will revive us after two days; on the third day he will raise us up, that we may live in his presence" (Hos 6:2). The death described in this text is real. Israel does indeed perish in the wilderness of exile, but God raises his people back up and returns them to the land he has given them. A similar thought appears in Zechariah 10:9: "Though I sow them among the nations, in the distant places they will remember me, and they will stay alive with their children, and they will return." The metaphor of God sowing his seed among the nations indicates that though God's people have been scattered—and broken open in death upon the ground of the nations—God revives them, so that through their death, they spring forth into new life. Within the Minor Prophets, the concept of God draw-ing life out of death for Israel stands as Habakkuk's front and rear guard.

In summary, Habakkuk teaches that when God's loyal people embrace his vision, trust him, and live faithfully before him, they will experience life. This is true whether the nuance of "life" focuses on resto-ration through judgment or on resurrection. We close this section with a quote from the German pastor Christoph Friedrich Blumhardt that captures God's faithfulness and the expected fidelity from his people:

> God approaches us as a loving Father, and thus he is no longer some great, high, un-approachable, and inscrutable Being. He is

a fatherly protector wherever we go. From within us, our faith responds to the Father— and faith is no more than holding tight to the love that we, as children, have received from the Father.[2]

Habakkuk 2:2-5 and the New Testament

It goes almost without saying that Habakkuk 2:4 is foundational for Christian theology. This verse stands out for a number of reasons. In both Jewish and Christian traditions it becomes an orienting point to the life of faith before God. For Jews, this text has been identified as the distillation of the entire law.

> **SUMMARIZING PRINCIPLE**
>
> Rabbi Simlai in the third or fourth century AD suggested that all 613 precepts in the Torah had been reduced to 11 by King David (e.g., Psa 15), to 6 by Isaiah (Isa 33:15–16), to 3 by Micah (Mic 6:8), to 2 by Isaiah (Isa 56:1), and to 1 by Amos (Amos 5:4). It is worth noting that Habakkuk in 2:4 also based the whole teaching of the Torah on a single principle: "The righteous shall live by his faith."[3]

This verse also crystallizes the heart of the gospel. J. C. Beker states that "Hab. 2:4 is the crucial Old Testament text for Paul," as evidenced in Romans 1:17 and Galatians 3:11.[4] Nor may we forget its value for Hebrews 10:36–39, as I shall explore below. Still today, many Christians live under the burdens of persecution and oppression. But Christians are also those who await a new world, the heavenly city. We live in patient trust, awaiting a reality that is yet to be seen, made possible by our assurance of Christ's coming return.[5] Even as we wait with baited breath for Jesus to come back and make "all things new" (Rev 21:5), we live by faith in God—a faith that defines and permeates the whole of life.

Habakkuk 2:4 is quoted in Romans 1:17, Galatians 3:11, and Hebrews 10:36–39, though not exactly as it appears in the Old Testament. For this reason, there is some question as to how the New Testament writers read the text. Romans 1:17 and Galatians 3:11 both render Habakkuk 2:4 as some variation on "the righteous shall live by faith" (ESV), depending on translation. Hebrews 10:37–38 is nuanced differently: "Yet a little while, and the coming one will come and will not delay; but my righteous one shall live by faith, and if he shrinks back, my soul has no pleasure in him" (ESV).

> Even as we wait with baited breath for Jesus to come back and make "all things new" (Rev 21:5), we live by faith in God—a faith that defines and permeates the whole of life.

Who is the righteous one in Romans 1:17 and Galatians 3:11? It is possible to argue that the reference is to none other than the Messiah, Jesus Christ—the very demonstration of the "righteousness of God" mentioned in Romans 1:17a. This interpretation is attractive in many ways. It makes sense in terms of the identification of Jesus by the writer of Hebrews as the "coming one" (Heb 10:37). But it is more likely that the referent for the "righteous" of Romans 1:17, Galatians 3:11, and Hebrews 10:38 is the faithful follower of God, who trusts in God's salvation to the end, without shrinking back.

For the New Testament writers, the climax of God's acts of salvation, the pinnacle of the mighty work of God, is the finished work of Jesus Christ, his Son. Stuhlmacher is helpful on this point, and it is worthwhile to quote him at length:

> Paul made the expression "the righteousness of God" the center of the gospel in that, together with the Christians before and beside him, he spoke of God's salvific activity for the sinful world in and through Christ and related God's righteousness strictly to faith. Through faith in Jesus Christ as redeemer and Lord, every individual Jew and Gentile obtains a positive share in the work of the one, just God who brings forth through Jesus Christ peace, salvation, and deliverance for Israel, the Gentile nations, and the (nonhuman) creation.[6]

Indeed, "the righteousness of God" finds its climax in the gospel of Jesus Christ. God gave Jesus so that humanity might be reconciled to himself; he offers forgiveness through repentance from sin and belief in Jesus as Messiah and Lord. Those who embrace Jesus are declared "righteous" in the sight of God and find new life, both now and through eternity. They live faithfully before their Maker in and through the whole of life. Those who embrace Christ in faith, then, are righteous and will live. The birth, death, resurrection, and second coming of Jesus comprise the substance of God's faithfulness.

There is no possibility of obtaining life through any means other than Jesus. The question of how a person could be saved and attain life loomed large for Paul in the context of his writing to the Galatian church. Is it possible, these believers wanted to know, to receive life through any means other than Jesus? Some Jews in the Galatian church believed that salvation might be earned through detailed observance of Old Testament law (what Paul calls "works of the law") *in addition* to, or in conjunction with, belief in Jesus. The glaring problem is that observance of the law has *never* managed to solve the sin problem in the hearts and lives of humankind. Paul reminds the church that it is solely by faith in God's faithfulness that one may obtain forgiveness and life. God gave Jesus *for life*, and to obtain life, the righteous must express their allegiance to God through repentance of their sin and faith in Jesus. It is precisely in doing so that the righteous shall live by faith (Gal 3:11).

> The birth, death, resurrection, and second coming of Jesus comprise the substance of God's faithfulness.

But expressing allegiance to Jesus through belief in and obedience to him demands that the fires of faith be stoked—the point of Hebrews 10:36–39. The context of this passage is that some believers were in danger of falling away or shrinking back from their initial commitment to Jesus. The writer of Hebrews reminds the Church that Jesus is coming back to judge the living and the dead ("the coming one will come and will not delay"). In the meantime, God's people are to live faithfully before him ("my righteous one shall live by faith, and if he shrinks back, my soul has no pleasure in him").[7] The prophecy of Habakkuk becomes for the writer of Hebrews a means to encourage God's people to be faithful to the end. We need this word of encouragement as well!

SUGGESTED READING

- ☐ Habakkuk 2
- ☐ Romans 1
- ☐ Galatians 3
- ☐ Hebrews 10:36–39; 12:1–2

Reflection

How does Habakkuk 2:2–5 express God's faithfulness? What does this mean to you?

_____

_____

_____

_____

Does it make you uncomfortable that translators and New Testament authors interpret the prophet's pivotal words in Habakkuk 2:4 so differently from one another? Could some of these interpretations be wrong, or might they suggest different nuances of truth, all of them legitimate?

_____

_____

_____

_____

In what ways do you find yourself tempted to shrink back from faithfulness to God? What encouragement does the Word of the Lord in Hebrews 10:36–39 afford you?

_____

_____

_____

_____

HABAKKUK AND JESUS

Introduction

> This man is the secret of heaven and earth,
> of the cosmos created by God (Karl Barth,
> CD III/1, 21).

Jesus is the clue that unlocks the "mystery" of creation. Paul reminds the Colossian church that Christ is the image of the invisible God and the firstborn over all of creation (Col 1:15). All things are made through him and for him, and all must return to him. The renowned German pastor and theologian Dietrich Bonhoeffer captured the magnitude of Jesus as follows:

> He is the centre and the strength of the Bible,
> of the Church, and of theology, but also of
> humanity, of reason, of justice and of cul-
> ture. Everything must return to Him; it is
> only under His protection that it can live.[1]

If this is true, how does Habakkuk "return" to Jesus? In this section we will turn our gaze from

Scripture to Jesus and back again. In so doing, we will see Jesus afresh through the prophecy of Habakkuk.

Jesus and the Righteousness of God

Habakkuk is concerned with God's people surviving calamity. He questions how long evil will persist in his world and what God will do about the sin problem. God's response is unequivocal: He will right all of the world's wrongs. He will judge his people because of their sin but will ultimately grant them life on the basis of his righteous deliverance. He will make all things new.

This is a key theme in Habakkuk, but more than that, it is central to biblical theology. God's deliverance and restoration constitute a major theme in the Old Testament prophets, often centered upon the concept of Zion. We see this, for instance, in Isaiah 2:1-4 and Micah 4:1-5. The theme also appears in the beautiful restoration oracles of Isaiah 60-62 and 65:17-25. This language is picked up in the New Testament as well, where Jesus is portrayed as God's agent of change in the world—as the One who "reconciles" all things back to God, as the apostle Paul puts it in Colossians 1:15-20. We also see this motif of the restoration of all things in the well-worn (but ever fresh) phrasing of the Apostle John:

> For in this way God loved the world, so that he gave his one and only Son, in order that everyone who believes in him will not perish, but will have eternal life. For God did not send his Son into the world in order that he should judge the world, but in order

that the world should be saved through him (John 3:16–17).

Bible scholar Tom Wright has a unique way of expressing this: He asserts that the entirety of Scripture testifies to a God who loves the world and wants to "put the world to rights."[2] God's plan, as revealed in his Word, is to set *right* a world that has gone terribly wrong due to human sin. God's actions of deliverance for Israel testify that his divine plan is coming true: The "righteousness of God" is on display. But the New Testament clarifies that all of the former acts of deliverance pointed to *the ultimate, final, and consummate* act of salvation: the "righteousness of God" fully showcased in the sending of his Son, Jesus Christ.

It is entirely appropriate to understand Jesus as the ultimate demonstration of God's faithfulness to his people anticipated in Habakkuk 2. The Old Greek translation of Habakkuk 2:4 highlights the faithfulness of God to set right the world's wrongs: "If he draws back, my soul is not pleased in him; but the righteous one will live by my faithfulness" (author's translation). God is worthy of our fidelity precisely because of his extraordinary divine faithfulness, both in guaranteeing the vision of Habakkuk (2:2–3) and in guaranteeing the coming of Christ the Lord.

> The New Testament clarifies that all of the former acts of deliverance pointed to the ultimate, final, and consummate act of salvation: the "righteousness of God" fully showcased in the sending of his Son, Jesus Christ.

Hope for Today

Jesus is the ultimate fulfillment of Habakkuk's longing for justice. God provides his vision to assuage Habakkuk's concerns, giving him hope for living in the present. As we have seen, after God encourages Habakkuk to live by faith, trusting in him and in the vision of vindication from 2:6–20, the prophet responds with the radical affirmation of trust in Habakkuk 3.

A similar tension between God's word of vindication and its final consummation affects us today. In the light of Scripture, we know that God has given his word of ultimate salvation in Jesus Christ: The world is "saved through" Jesus (John 3:17). But the reception of Habakkuk 2:4 in Hebrews, as we have seen above, reminds us that although Jesus has already come once, he will come again. In the meantime, the Church looks to Jesus and beseeches in anticipation, "Come quickly, Lord Jesus!" The Church is called to look to Jesus with faith and trust, knowing that he has already accomplished all things necessary for our salvation. In the time between his ascension and his second coming we are called to live faithfully before him.

Living faithfully before the Lord is an exercise of hope. Hope arrives in the person of Jesus, who gives himself freely to those who are captured by his love. Hope, in this sense, is inherently relational, coming from a God who bounds toward us with infinite speed.[3] He is coming and will not delay—despite appearances in our time-bound reality—as the writer of Hebrews asserts. Our hope is in God.

To what or whom, then, shall we cling? The book of Habakkuk reminds us that our hope is in the Father,

This hope is neither empty nor vain, and it carries us forward, regardless of circumstances, into each new day.

the God who saves and delivers, but it is also in God's Son, Jesus Christ, who has come and is coming again, and in the Holy Spirit, who binds us together in unity and mission, guiding us to truth and comforting us in our affliction. This hope is neither empty nor vain, and it carries us forward, regardless of circumstances, into each new day.

> For in hope we were saved, but hope that is seen is not hope, for who hopes for what he sees? But if we hope for what we do not see, we await it eagerly with patient endurance (Rom 8:24–25).

> Yet I will rejoice in Yahweh;
> I will exult in the God of my salvation.
> Yahweh, my Lord, is my strength;
> he makes my feet like the deer;
> he causes me to walk on my high places (Hab 3:18–19).

SUGGESTED READING

☐   Habakkuk 2:4

☐   Romans 1; Galatians 3; Hebrews 10:37–39

☐   John 3:16–17

☐   Romans 8

Reflection

Consider once again the quote from Dietrich Bonhoeffer: "[Jesus] is the centre and the strength of the Bible, of the Church, and of theology, but also of humanity, of reason, of justice and of culture. Everything must return to Him; it is only under His protection that it can live." How are Bonhoeffer's thoughts significant for your understanding of Jesus? How do they encourage you?

_____

_____

_____

_____

Where do you find Jesus in the teaching of Habakkuk?

_____

_____

_____

_____

To what or whom do you cling for hope? Friendship? Family? Possessions? Reflect on what it means for you personally that Jesus is our hope.

_____

_____

_____

_____

_____

CONCLUSION

We turn again to Voltaire's grudge against the prophet Habakkuk: Is this rogue capable of *anything worthwhile*? I hope this study has revealed Habakkuk not as a loose canon but as a helpful doorway into renewed vitality in the house of faith. The book unpacks for us what it means to suffer, pray, and hope in God. It also leads us to Christ, the center and strength of Scripture.

Habakkuk provides for us a spirituality of complaint that is deeply dependent upon God and expressive of trust in God's goodness. While others in the world may have it worse than we do, we have to wrestle with our own pain, whatever its degree, authentically and fully before our God. Minimizing or deflecting suffering is not a healthy coping mechanism. Suffering cannot be plastered over; it must be dealt with, and Habakkuk provides a model of doing just that—through active and honest *prayer to God*.

> Habakkuk provides for us a spirituality of complaint that is deeply dependent upon God and expressive of trust in God's goodness.

When facing tough times, the Church may respond through philosophical and systematic-theological explanations for why suffering exists and how a good God might be squared with massive amounts of human angst. This is a very real issue in our world today, one that leads too many away from the faith.

Addressing in such a manner the paradox of a good God in conjunction with human suffering is no doubt instructive and necessary, but Habakkuk provides a different valence to the question. The book approaches its experiential side: How does an individual or community *cope* with the experience of suffering when a rational explanation will not suffice? Habakkuk affords a word of hope in that God is in the business of righting wrongs and suffering. More important, Habakkuk provides a model for coping with suffering through prayer.

I find it encouraging that Jesus took the same tactic on the night of his suffering in the garden of Gethsemane. Declining to sit by and wait for some other means of dealing with his pain, our Lord took his burdens directly to his Father. In light of Habakkuk's suggestion of the model of Jesus, 1 Peter 5:7 comes alive in a new way: We are to cast our cares upon the Lord "because he cares" for us. Followers of Jesus would do well to emulate Habakkuk by being "devoted to prayer" (Rom 12:12; Col 4:2). Prayer is the first and best reflex of the Church.

> Prayer is the first and best reflex of the Church.

As we conclude this volume on Habakkuk, reflect on these words:

For the earth will be filled
with the knowledge of the glory of Yahweh,
like the waters covering the sea (Hab 2:14).

We have the assurance that the earth *will indeed* be filled with the knowledge of the glory of the Lord. As Paul enthused to the Philippian Christians:

Therefore also God exalted him [Jesus]
and graciously granted him the name above
every name,
so that at the name of Jesus
every knee should bow,
of *those* in heaven and of *those* on earth and
of *those* under the earth,
and every tongue confess
that Jesus Christ *is* Lord,
to the glory of God the Father (Phil 2:9–11).

As the gospel of Jesus Christ advances in the world, Paul's words come increasingly to fruition. And yet those words await the fullness of Habakkuk's vision in 2:14, the day when the whole earth will be *filled* (to bursting, we might say) with the glory of God. But in the meantime, how are believers to live? Habakkuk gives an answer:

Faith: Trust in the faithfulness of God and live faithfully before him.

Hope: Wait on the Lord with expectancy. Our hope is real and legitimate.

To these two habits of life for the believer we could add one more:

Love: Position love for God and neighbor as the front and rear guard of your life.

Reflection

How has this study on Habakkuk impacted your life? Be as specific as you can.

Do you find it more helpful to reflect philosophically or theologically on the problem of pain or to accept its reality and focus on healthy, God-honoring coping strategies?

How has your approach to suffering and pain in the Christian life changed in light of what you've learned from Habakkuk?

RECOMMENDED READING FOR HABAKKUK

Donald E. Gowan. *The Triumph of Faith in Habakkuk.* Atlanta, GA: John Knox Press, 1976.

- A dated but still useful theological commentary.

Faustin Ntamushobora. *From Trials to Triumphs: The Voice of Habakkuk to the Suffering African Christian.* Eugene, OR: Wipf & Stock, 2009.

- A reading of Habakkuk tooled for the African community.

Heath A. Thomas. *Habakkuk.* Two Horizons Old Testament Commentary. Grand Rapids, MI: Eerdmans, (forthcoming).

- My commentary on the book of Habakkuk, which focuses on exegetical detail and theological interpretation. I further touch on the New Testament use of Habakkuk and Habakkuk's prophecy as it relates to Jesus.

Heath A. Thomas. "Hearing the Minor Prophets: The Book of the Twelve and God's Address." In *Hearing the Old Testament: Listening for God's Address.* Edited by Craig G. Bartholomew and David H. Beldman. Grand Rapids, MI: Eerdmans, 2012.

- In this commentary, I provide an overview of the major theological themes of the Minor Prophets and their relation to Jesus and the New Testament.

NOTES

Chapter 1: Introduction

1. I have translated from the French. The original reads: "Monsieur, vous ne connoissez guères ce Habacouc; ce coquin est capable de tout!" French quotation from Friedrich August Gottreu Tholuck, "On the Hypothesis of the Egyptian or Indian Origin of the Name Jehovah," *Biblical Repository* 4/13 (1834): 92-93, note 3.

2. Gary V. Smith, *The Prophets as Preachers: An Introduction to the Hebrew Prophets* (Nashville, TN: B&H Academic, 1994), 179.

3. See Bill T. Arnold, *Who Were the Babylonians?* (Archaeology and Biblical Studies 10; Leiden: Brill, 2005/Atlanta: Society of Biblical Literature, 2004), 87-105. For a timeline of historical events related to Habakkuk, see pp. 91-105. For specific dates, see J. Maxwell Miller and John H. Hayes, *A History of Ancient Israel and Judah* (2d ed.; London: SCM Press, 1986), 383-415.

4. Peter Stuhlmacher, *Paul's Letter to the Romans: A Commentary* (Louisville, KY: Westminster John Knox, 1994), 188.

5. Faustin Ntamushobora, *From Trials to Triumphs: The Voice of Habakkuk to the Suffering African Christian* (Eugene, OR: Wipf & Stock, 2009).

Chapter 2: Prophecy in the Bible

1. See Eric Seibert, *Disturbing Divine Behavior: Troubling Old Testament Images of God* (Minneapolis, MN: Fortress Press, 2009). For a helpful approach to divine violence and wrath, see David T. Lamb, *God Behaving Badly: Is the God of the Old Testament Angry, Sexist and Racist?* (Downers Grove, IL: Inter-Varsity Press, 2011).

2. Hal Lindsay, *The Late Great Planet Earth* (Grand Rapids, MI: Zondervan, 1970), first lines of the introduction.

3. For Jesus' fulfillment of the Suffering Servant prophecy, see: Bernd Janowski and Peter Stuhlmacher (eds.), *The Suffering Servant: Isaiah 53 in Jewish and Christian Sources* (Grand Rapids, MI: Eerdmans, 2004); and Darrell L. Bock and Mitch Glaser (eds.), *The Gospel According to Isaiah 53: Encountering the Suffering Servant in Jewish and Christian Theology* (Grand Rapids, MI: Kregel Academic, 2012).

4. For discussion on Jesus as a prophet, see Ben Witherington III, *Jesus the Seer: The Progress of Prophecy* (Minneapolis, MN: Fortress Press, 2014), 329–50.

Chapter 3: A Portrait of Habakkuk

1. C. C. Torrey, *The Lives of the Prophets: Greek Text and Translation* (JBLMS 1; Philadelphia: Society of Biblical Literature and Exegesis, 1946), 43–44.

2. Bernard Shaw, *John Bull's Other Island and Major Barbara* (New York: Brentano's, 1911), xxxii.

3. This is from Midrash Psalms 7:17, quoted in Hayyim Angel, "Biblical Prayers and Rabbinic Responses: Balancing Truthfulness and Respect Before God," *JBQ* 38/1 (2010), 3–9 (4).

4. Angel, "Biblical Prayers."

5. J. F. A. Sawyer, *Prophecy and Prophets of the Old Testament*, OBS (Oxford: Oxford University Press, 1987), 119. He is speaking of the supposed oracle of hearing that is given by the cultic prophet after a lament or complaint has been uttered.

6. Ntamushobora, *From Trials to Triumphs*.

Chapter 4: Habakkuk's View of God

1. John Calvin, *Institutes of the Christian Religion* (trans. Henry Beveridge; Peabody, MA: Hendrickson, 2008): §I.6.1, 26–27.

2. Charles H. Spurgeon, "World on Fire (Sermon 1125)," in *The Metropolitan Tabernacle Pulpit: Containing Sermons Preached and Revised*, Volume 19 (Pasadena, TX: Pilgrim Publications, 1969), 433–45 (438).

Chapter 5: Prophecy and Poetry

1. Samuel A. Meier, *Themes and Transformations in Old Testament Prophecy* (Downers Grove, IL: IVP Academic, 2009), 82–86.

Chapter 6: Waiting on God

1. See the renowned work by Richard J. Foster, *The Celebration of Discipline: The Path to Spiritual Growth* (San Francisco, CA: Harper San Francisco, 2006).

2. Martin Laird, *Into the Silent Land: A Guide to the Christian Practice of Contemplation* (Oxford: Oxford University Press, 2006), 2.

3. Lord Alfred Tennyson, "In Memoriam A.H.H.," in M. H. Abrams (ed.), *The Norton Anthology of English Literature* (6th ed.; vol. 2; New York: W.W. Norton and Company, 1993), 1105.

Chapter 7: Faith in the Faithful God

1. Stuhlmacher, *Paul's Letter to the Romans*, 30.

2. Christoph Friedrich Blumhardt, *The Gospel of God's Reign: Living for the Kingdom of God.* Edited by C. T. Collins and C. E. Moore (Eugene, OR: Cascade, 2014), 9.

3. Babylonian Talmud, Tractate Makkoth: §23b–24a.

4. J. Christiaan Beker, "Echoes and Intertextuality," in *Paul and the Scriptures of Israel*, JNTSup, 83. Edited by Craig A. Evans and James A. Sanders (Sheffield: JSOT Press, 1993), 64–69 (68).

5. See the discussion of R. Coggins and J. H. Han, *Six Minor Prophets Through the Centuries: Nahum, Habakkuk, Zephaniah, Haggai, Zechariah and Malachi*, BBC (London: Wiley-Blackwell, 2011), 71–73.

6. Stuhlmacher, *Paul's Letter to the Romans*, 31.

7. See the excellent discussion of Peter T. O'Brien, *The Letter to the Hebrews* (PNTC; Nottingham, UK: Apollos/Grand Rapids, MI: Eerdmans, 2010), 387–93.

Chapter 8: Habakkuk and Jesus

1. Dietrich Bonhoeffer, *Ethics* (trans. N. H. Smith; New York: Macmillan, 1965), 56.

2. N. T. Wright, *Simply Christian: Why Christianity Makes Sense* (New York: HarperOne, 2006), 10, 37, 75, 78, 79, and 235.

3. The phrase comes from C. S. Lewis, *Miracles* (New York: Fount, 1974), 98.

Printed in the United States
by Baker & Taylor Publisher Services